"*Managing Knock Your Socks Off Service* gets two thumbs up, three likes, and five stars! A must-read for all customer-focused leaders."

—M.E. Castillo, CEO
Arbor Company

"Este libro es sin duda una excelente herramienta que permite a los líderes empresariales alinear su estrategia de negocio, centrándola en el cliente, que es el verdadero éxito en cualquier negocio." (This book is an excellent tool to help managers align their thought processes to be able to structure a successful customer-centric business.)"

—Juan Carlos Arguello, CEO
Banco de Finanzas (Nicaragua)

"*Managing Knock Your Socks Off Service* is a powerful source of insights, ideas, and action plans that will lead your team to uplifting service!"

—Ron Kaufman, *New York Times* best-selling author
Uplifting Service

"In an era where organizations must seek new ways to differentiate themselves, *Managing Knock Your Socks Off Service* is an uplifting and compelling reminder of the impact a well-defined culture has on the bottom line."

—Lani Hayward, EVP of Creative Strategies
Umpqua Bank

"Consistently excellent service is only as good as it is deliberately managed. Bell and Zemke masterfully guide how to accomplish this feat with distinction."

—Jeanne Bliss, best-selling author
Chief Customer Officer and
I Love You More Than My Dog

"The authors give valuable insights—backed up with case studies—on how to turn every customer into a customer for life."

—*Entrepreneur Magazine*

"A lively and timely book written for anyone who deals with customers."

—Jane Applegate, nationally syndicated columnist

Managing Knock Your Socks Off Service

3rd Edition

By Chip R. Bell and Ron Zemke

American Management Association

New York • Atlanta • Brussels • Chicago • Mexico City • San Francisco
Shanghai • Tokyo • Toronto • Washington, D.C.

Library of Congress Cataloging-in-Publication Data

Bell, Chip R.
  Managing knock your socks off service / Chip R. Bell and Ron Zemke.—Third Edition.
      pages cm
      Includes bibliographical references and index.
    ISBN-13: 978-0-8144-3204-4
    ISBN-10: 0-8144-3204-4
    1. Customer services. I. Zemke, Ron. II. Title.
  HF5415.5.B436 2013
  658.8'12—dc23   *2012034663*

About AMA
*American Management Association (www.amanet.org) is a world
leader in talent development, advancing the skills of individuals to
drive business success. Our mission is to support the goals of
individuals and organizations through a complete range of products
and services, including classroom and virtual seminars, webcasts,
webinars, podcasts, conferences, corporate and government solutions,
business books and research. AMA's approach to improving performance
combines experiential learning—learning through doing—with opportunities
for ongoing professional growth at every step of one's career journey.*

Printing number

10 9 8 7 6 5 4 3 2 1

Contents

Preface   vii

Thanks   xi

Imperative 1: Find and Retain Quality People   **1**

  1 Recruit Creatively and Hire Carefully   3
  2 Keeping Your Best and Brightest   12

Imperative 2: Know Your Customers Intimately   **19**

  3 Why Customer Satisfaction Isn't Enough   21
  4 Listening Is a Contact Sport   28
  5 A Complaining Customer Is Your
     Best Friend   38
  6 Little Things Mean a Lot   46
  7 Learning from Lost Customers   54

Imperative 3: Build a Service Vision   **59**

  8 The Power of a Service Strategy   61
  9 Getting Your Vision Down on Paper   70
 10 Service Standards Build Consistency   77

**Imperative 4: Make Your Service Delivery Processes
ETDBW (Easy to Do Business With)**   **85**

 11 Effort: The Achilles' Heel of Customer
     Experience   87
 12 Making Service Delivery Processes
     "Happy"   94
 13 Measure and Manage from the Customer's
     Point of View   102
 14 Serving Online: When Clicks
     Replace Bricks   111
 15 Add Magic: Creating the Unpredictable and
     Unique   120
 16 Make Recovery a Point of Pride   127

Imperative 5:   Train and Coach   **135**

   17   Start on Day One (When Their Hearts
           and Minds Are Malleable)   137
   18   Training Creates Competence, Confidence,
           and Commitment to Customers   144
   19   Thinking and Acting Like a Coach   151

Imperative 6:   Involve, Empower, and Inspire   **161**

   20   Fostering Responsible Freedom   163
   21   Removing the Barriers to Empowerment   170
   22   Inspiring Passion for the Customer   177

**Imperative 7:   Recognize, Reward, Incent,
                   and Celebrate**   **183**

   23   Recognition and Reward: Fueling the
           Fires of Service Success   185
   24   Feedback: Breakfast, Lunch, and Dinner
           of Champions   190
   25   The Art of Interpersonal Feedback   196
   26   Incenting Great Service   201
   27   Celebrate Success   204

Imperative 8:   Set the Tone and Lead the Way   **211**

   28   Great Service Leaders Foster Trust   213
   29   Great Service Leadership in Action   218

       Endnotes   225

       Index   229

       About the Authors   237

Preface

Has customer service gotten worse, or have we just become a nation of gripers and whiners?

My father was a big fan of the comic strip *Mutt and Jeff.* His favorite had Mutt and Jeff enjoying a bit of verbal sparring. "If everyone saw like I did," boasted Jeff, "Everyone would want my wife." "If everyone saw like I did," quipped Mutt, "*No one* would want your wife."

It was my first lesson on the "eye of the beholder" side of understanding relationships and human experiences. So, when someone asked me the question at the top of the page, I thought about my dad's favorite joke.

Remember the scene in the movie *Back to the Future* when a customer pulls into a gas station circa the 1950s and two squeaky clean attendants cheerfully wash the windshield and carefully check the engine fluids? Audiences laughed at the obvious spoof.

Was that great customer service? I don't remember thinking that it was back in the 50s and 60s. It was just neighborly care by local employees with the luxury of being able to serve one customer at a time. They worked for an enterprise with reasonably healthy profit margins, friendly competitors, and freedom from having to deal with litigious consumers, restrictive regulations, or impatient shareholders. They served customers with limited choices, modest expectations, and fewer time constraints.

Fast forward to today. Customer care has been crowded to the back of the line by a host of familiar pressures. Profit margins have been squeezed by global competitors, convincing more executives to compete on operational efficiency and becoming low-cost providers. Cost-containment became the watchword, leading to wholesale outsourcing of customer service functions to low-wage, off-shore call centers, reduction of customers' toll-free phone access, driving customers to automation and self-service, slashing of value-adding amenities, and making service training for frontline employees an afterthought rather than a necessity.

The gradual erosion of personal care and attention in the service experience has had predictable consequences. According to recent research by American Express, nine in ten Americans (91 percent) consider the level of customer service important when deciding to do business with a company. But only 24 percent of Americans believe companies value their business and will go the extra mile to keep it.[1] A report from RightNow Technologies (now a part of Oracle) and Harris Interactive indicates that 82 percent of consumers in the United States said they've *stopped* doing business with a company due to a poor customer service experience. Ninety-five percent of customers said that after a bad customer experience they would "take action."[2]

Yet there are signs of hope amidst the rage. More companies across industries have rediscovered a simple but powerful truth about creating distinction in their markets: Consistently treat customers like they are unique and special, and it will quickly set the company apart from the mass of others competing solely on price and offering unresponsive or indifferent service. Part of the impetus for attention to the customer is social media. With more than five times the influence power, word of mouse (or touchpad) trumps word of mouth. Today, a tweet, blog post, or YouTube video gone viral can overnight bring a successful organization to its knees. Wise organizations realize that by crafting processes, practices, and policies that play fair with customers, allow people to feel heard and respected when there are problems, and create the feeling that customers' best interests are being looked after, they build the ultimate competitive weapon: the fervently loyal customer who evangelizes to all within earshot (or Internet connection) about their organization.

More leaders are also being won over by the continuing stream of evidence that shows the correlation between engaged employees and happy customers—and the indisputable link between happy customers and healthy profits. Studies done by economists and service researchers leave little doubt: Companies rated high on the quality of their customer service regularly keep customers longer, have lower sales and marketing costs (as a result of not having to continually replace customers who've defected due to poor service), and often experience higher return on sales.

So what do Zappos.com, Nordstrom, Starbucks, Amazon, and USAA know that Mayday Airlines, Woeful Healthcare, and Sam's Pretty Decent Car Repair still seem clueless about?

We have studied the service greats for many years. Prior to his untimely death in 2004, Ron Zemke (who coauthored the first edition of this book) conducted pioneering research on the service leadership practices consistently found in companies known for service excellence. His studies encompassed thousands of managers in hundreds of companies. Enriched and corroborated by research conducted by others, Ron's massive body of work forms the foundation of the principles and practices found in this book.

If we've learned one thing from the thousands of managers with whom we have worked in ferreting out the keys to successful service experiences, it is this: Start with good people or else don't even start. It takes bright, savvy, well-trained, and emotionally resilient front liners to make your service vision a dream come true.

Once you've found them, of course, you have to work hard to keep them. Much of that responsibility falls on your shoulders. Study after study shows that employees leave organizations primarily because of poor relationships with managers, not because of pay, benefits, or other factors. How well you train, coach, empower, and support your people— and whether you show appreciation for the hard work they do each day in the trenches serving customers—makes all the difference not only in retaining your best employees, but also in creating memorable experiences for customers.

Yes, the other factors (which we refer to as operational imperatives) are important. But those factors assume that you have hired people capable of doing, and who are willing to do, the job, people who are eager to learn and excited about the idea of helping you create a special organization—an organization distinguished by Knock Your Socks Off Service.

So what do you think? Has customer service gotten better, or is there still a long way for most organizations to go? How

that question is answered will depend largely on what you
and your colleagues do tomorrow, and all of the challenging
and exciting days that follow, to create the conditions that
enable your frontline people to consistently delight and amaze
customers.

Chip R. Bell
October 2012

Thanks

"Thank you" is a phrase we use with a myriad of emotions and a variety of depth. The phrase can be as ordinary as the words we use when we get our order at the drive-in window of a fast-food restaurant. The exact same phrase can be as overwhelming as the farewell to a departing parent at graveside.

This is the place in the book we reserve to say "thank you." And, we try to find a way to express it so that it really, really matters. The task is a bit daunting, not unlike all those Academy Award winners whom we annually watch struggle under spotlight and camera to remember all the people to thank.

The most important person to thank is the spiritual coauthor of this book, the late Ron Zemke. We had so much fun crafting the first edition. I was perpetually awed and blessed by his wit, wisdom, and wonderful friendship. He was very passionate about writing—-toiling long and late over the precise way to express what we were trying to communicate. Language was his canvas, and he was an extraordinary artist. I deeply miss his presence but never take for granted his influence. Thank you, Z Man!

We are lifelong learners in this business of service. Since customers are forever changing, the path to excellence is clearly a journey, not a destination. We thank our clients who continue to teach us through their struggles, failures, and triumphs. They have challenged us to remember that the client's enthusiasm is too often dampened by the consultant's wisdom. They remind us that humility and courage are the primary traits of pioneers.

Jill Applegate was our detail manager extraordinaire through all the editions. She always kept us on task and relentlessly served as the reader who kept us relevant and timely. We could not have done this work without her. Her work was particularly beneficial on this third edition. The late John Bush never ceased to amaze us with his "capture the essence" creative illustrations.

Finally, we owe a special thanks to Nancy Rainey Bell and Susan Zemke, who not only gave emotional sustenance, compassionate critique, and undying love, but frequently "took up the slack" to provide valuable space for focus on this book.

To all of you: Thanks.

Imperative 1
Find and Retain Quality People

Hire good people and work like heck to keep them on the payroll. Knock Your Socks Off Service starts here or it doesn't start at all.

If you are really serious about serving customers better than your competition, you have to start with people who are willing and able to make that happen. Hiring well means being downright picky about who works under your flag. When it comes to creating and maintaining a positive relationship with customers, hiring *nobody* is sometimes better than settling for the first warm body that volunteers to show up for eight hours. You can't end up with loyal customers if you don't start with quality people—the kind of people who get as big a kick out of delivering great service as customers do receiving it. Period.

You've really recruited some super people this time.

c BUSH

But this is a two-act play. Once found and brought on board, quality people must be kept on board. That means orienting them carefully so they come to understand just exactly what you mean by high-quality service. It also means training them fully in the knowledge and skills necessary for success, giving them challenging assignments, and keeping them interested in the work of the organization. And sometimes it means paying them better than (and/or differently than) the competition is willing to.

It also means growing them, rewarding and recognizing their accomplishments—sometimes individually, sometimes as a team. It means celebrating their efforts when they go "one step beyond" for their customers.

If you seriously intend to distinguish yourself from the competition through smooth, seamless Knock Your Socks Off Service, you won't accomplish that by hiring from the labor pool from hell or by maintaining a payroll that turns over faster than dishwashers in a Las Vegas hotel.

1

Recruit Creatively and Hire Carefully

Development can help great people be even better—but if I had a dollar to spend, I'd spend 70 cents getting the right person in the door.

—Paul Russell
Director of Leadership and
Development, Google

On Interstate 4 southwest of Orlando, Florida, a striking cream and tan building fronts the freeway. A big—very big—sign defines it in one eloquently simple word: casting. It's the Walt Disney World personnel office. That one word says a lot about not just Disney but all companies that are focused on becoming known for Knock Your Socks Off Service. They don't "hire" people for "jobs" in an organization; they "cast" people for a "role" in a service performance.

In service-focused companies, customer service jobs are thought of less like factory work and much more like theater. At a play, the audience files in, the curtain goes up, the actors make their entrances and speak their lines, and—if each and every cast member, not to mention the writer, director, stagehands, costumers, makeup artists, and lighting technicians, has prepared themselves and the theater well—the audience enjoys the show and tells others about it. Then again, the whole production can be a magnificent flop if just one person fails to do a job on which everyone else depends.

In today's service-driven business world, you are more director than boss, more choreographer than administrator. Your frontline people are the actors, and your customers are the audience for whom they must perform. Everyone else is support crew, charged with making sure the theater is right, the sets ready, and the actors are primed and prepared. You have to prepare your cast to know their cues, hit their marks, deliver their lines, and improvise when another cast member or someone in the audience disrupts the carefully plotted flow of the performance. And, of course, once the curtain goes up, all you can do is watch and whisper from the wings. You're not allowed on stage. You'd just get in the way!

Balancing Efficiency and Effectiveness

Given all the currents flowing under and around the hiring process today, the last thing you want to do is rush into a decision that can make or break how the critics—your customers—rate the quality of your service performances. Once the casting decision has been made, your entire production's reviews are going to depend on the person you've chosen for the role. It's as easy to be taken in by an attractive external facade as by a well-proportioned résumé. Neither may be truly indicative of whether someone can play the part the way you need it to be played.

Yes, the show must go on. But if you've been building a good, versatile cast, you should have understudies ready to fill in while you look for new additions to your service repertory crew. Despite the pressures for output or scarcity of talent, don't rush the process. Invest the time and effort needed to get the right person. When you do, you'll find you're in good company.

In our research of companies with exemplary service practices, we found painstaking thoroughness built into every step of their selection process for service employees. Rather than focusing only on metrics like cost-per-hire or time-to-fill open jobs, these organizations were just as concerned with finding the right fit—in both an applicant's technical skills as well as hard-wired attributes like personality and values—for customer contact jobs. Customer-centric companies understand that success in service roles is as much about having the right temperament or the desire and emotional fortitude to deal with customers day in and out, as it is about product knowledge or mastering new technologies. While plenty of job prospects are blessed with good social skills, not all have a high level of *tolerance for contact*—the ability to engage in many successive short bursts of interaction with customers without becoming overstressed, robotic, or unempathetic.

Casting a Role, Not Filling a Job

Filling out your service cast with people who can star in their roles is the key to success. But casting your customer service play is far more involved and difficult than hiring "somebody—anybody" to sit in a chair and answer a phone or stand at a counter and take orders. Consider the following three key differences between merely filling a slot and finding someone capable of playing a part.

1. *Great service performers must be able to create a relationship with the audience.* From the customer's standpoint, every performance is "live" and hence unique. It earns the best reviews when it appears genuine, perhaps even spontaneous. And it should never be rigidly scripted—certainly not canned.

- *Implication*: Customer service cast members must have good person-to-person skills; their speaking, listening, and interacting styles should seem natural and friendly and appropriate to the situation—neither stiff and formal nor overly familiar. As Jim von Maur, president of Iowa-based Von Maur department stores, says of his own company's hiring philosophy, "My Dad had a theory: We can train them to sell. We can't train them to be nice—that was their parents' job."[3]

2. *Great service performers must be able to handle pressure.* There are many kinds of pressure—pressure of the

clock, pressure from customers, pressure from other players in the service cast, and pressure from the desire to do a good job for both customer and company even though the two may be in conflict.

- *Implication*: Members of the customer service cast must be good at handling their own emotions, be calm under fire, and not be susceptible to "catching the stress virus" from upset customers. At the same time, they have to acknowledge and support their customers' upsets and problems and demonstrate a desire to help resolve the situation in the best way possible.

3. *Great service performers must be able to learn new scripts.* They have to be flexible enough to adjust to changes in the cast and conditions surrounding them, make changes in their own performance as conditions warrant, and still seem natural and knowledgeable.

- *Implication*: Customer service cast members need to be lifelong learners—curious enough to learn from the environment, comfortable enough to be constantly looking for new ways to enhance their performance, and confident enough to indulge the natural curiosity to ask, "Why is that?" and poke around the organization to learn how things really work. Those who are comfortable with change and handle it well can be the most helpful to customers and need minimal hand holding from their managers.

To get the right kind of people for your company, you have to know (1) what you're looking for and (2) how to look for it.

Eight Tips for Casting Well

1. *Treat every vacancy like an open role in a play.* Define the service role you are auditioning people for in terms of the part the new cast members must play and how they'll have to relate to the other members in the cast. Make people skills and technical knowledge of equal importance in your hiring.

2. *Identify the skills needed for the role.* Once the interview begins, it's too late to start thinking about what you want to learn. Based on the job description and your knowledge of the role you are casting, what traits or personal attributes do you want new cast members to possess? Friendliness? Competence? Empathy? Creativity? Confidence? How will you judge the presence or absence of those traits to your satisfaction? Focus the various stages of the selection process on the real-world skills demanded by the part you're trying to fill.

3. *"Screen test" your applicants.* Try role-playing difficult customer situations with applicants or posing "what would you do if" questions based on the kinds of situations likely to occur on the job. You don't want to listen just for "right" or "wrong" answers. You can train them to use the right words later. Listen for orientation and attitude.

PetSmart, the Phoenix, Arizona based retailer of specialty pet products, decided to move interviews with job candidates from its back office to the sales floor as a way to better "screen test" their interpersonal skills. Managers now walk applicants around the store, periodically striking up conversations with shoppers and then stepping back to see how the applicant interacts with the customer. The company believes these impromptu "auditions" provide a valuable glimpse into how candidates would function on the job.[4] The Ritz-Carlton Hotel Company has found that the way applicants greet employees in the back (or heart) of the house—the kitchen, housekeeping, or security—will tell a lot about how the front of the house guests will be treated should the applicant be hired.

4. *Use multiple selection methods.* Remember test anxiety in school? Job applicants get it, too. Instead of sifting all applicants through one coarse screen, use a succession of fine ones to help you differentiate. Using a variety of methods also helps counter an overreliance on intuition or gut feel in the hiring process. As Guy Kawasaki, author of the best-selling book *Enchantment* and a major contributor to the early success of Apple Computer says, "the problem with intuition is that people only remember when their intuition was right—truth be told, their intuition was probably wrong as often as right."

Selection Questions

There are no magic questions that automatically illustrate an applicant's character and service outlook. But there are questions that work better than others at eliciting the kind of information you need in order to make an informed hiring decision. Here are a few to use or adapt:

- What does giving the customer "superior service" mean to you?
- Let me give you a typical customer service situation we get here at Acme. (Describe the situation.) How would you handle this type of situation? (Look for attitude, not the perfect solution.)
- Tell me about a time when you successfully balanced the best interests of the company with the best interests of a customer.
- We all get weary from time to time from the pressure of dealing with people. What do you do to renew yourself so you can stay "up," fresh, and enthusiastic on the job?
- I know I sometimes get uptight when I have to deal with an irate customer. You've had experience with difficult customers. Can you offer an example that shows how you might typically handle them?
- What do you like most about being in customer service?
- If you were asked to coach someone brand new to serving customers, what advice would you give that person? What "do's and don'ts" would you tell them?

Consider:

- *Multiple Interviews.* See your applicants more than once, each time with specific objectives in mind for the interview. In the first interview you're likely to encounter a highly prepared or scripted candidate, but by the second or third interview you'll begin to see more of the "real" person who will provide more revealing, high-quality information.

- *Peer Interviews.* In firms where teamwork is valued, it's not uncommon for cast members who will be working with whomever is hired to be trained to do short interviews of their own. Their viewpoints are highly functional. When the project has to be finished under the gun, the person *you're* hiring is someone *they'll* need to work with and depend on. Southwest Airlines will not hire an applicant to be a flight attendant unless the applicant has received an affirmative nod from a group of Southwest flight attendants.

- *Job-Validated Testing.* Tests that reflect the true nature of the job and assess the key skills needed to do it proficiently are valid, provided they're administered equally and fairly to everyone under consideration. Use them.

- *Job Previewing.* Let applicants spend some time seeing what they're getting themselves into. If they're serious, they'll find ways to better present their qualifications to you. If the job turns out to be something other than what they were expecting, they'll often save you the cost of a bad hire by deselecting themselves. For example, one previewing technique for call center job candidates is to play excerpts of real calls they're likely to receive from customers. Hearing the nature of these calls might cause a few candidates to "select out" of the job, even if they have the requisite skills or background to qualify.

- *Pay to Exit.* Zappos.com, after new hires have completed their extensive orientation to the company values, offers new hires $2,000 to leave. While only a small percentage take the offer, Zappos has found the investment helps ensure those who remain are more likely to be their type of employee. In the long run, it saves them money.

   5. *Consider nontraditional sources.* The traditional entry-level workforce is shrinking. But the proportion of Americans over the age of fifty is mushrooming. Shrewd organizations are taking advantage of this seismic demographic shift by hiring

more retired workers for service roles. With their vast institutional knowledge, calm demeanor under fire, and strong work ethic, people of this generation are often a good fit for customer contact jobs. Harley-Davidson, for example, hires back its own recently retired employees for part-time roles like calling customers to gauge how well the company has satisfied their needs and to solicit ideas on how to improve service. Because they know the company and its products so well, the retirees are able to "generate deeper customer insights while also reinforcing the Harley brand," according to management.[5]

6. *Recruit actively.* Good people may not always find you—often you have to find them. Where have your best people been coming from? Are there others back there equally ready and willing to do the job for you? When you encounter service workers who make a strong impression, don't be shy about handing them your business card and suggesting they get in touch the next time they're ready to make a change. Consider rewarding your people—pay 'em a bounty—for bringing in friends, former colleagues, or even relatives who are capable of filling roles in your company. It's often a cheaper and more effective way of finding good talent than using Internet job boards, newspaper ads, or other traditional recruiting tools.

7. *Hire people like the job, not like you.* It's very human to overlay your own personal beliefs, values, likes, and dislikes on the selection process, but it's seldom in the best interest of the customer to do so. Beware of the "cloning" effect, or the tendency to hire people who think, act, or look like you or share the same background as you. Remember the words of economist Leo Rosten: "First-rate men hire first-rate men. Second-rate men hire third-rate men." (We're sure he'd have said "people" if he said this today.)

8. *Review history with your head; review attitude with your heart.* Customer service is a performing art. You size a person up in a job interview or at a social gathering by what your instinct—your proverbial gut—tells you about that person. If your vibes are sending you "disconnect" signals, don't silence them just because you're impressed with an

applicant's resume, references, or silver-tongued responses to your questions. If you are getting an uneasy feeling about a prospect, the customer may just share the same reaction. Remember, whatever happens in the interview process is likely a microcosm of what that person will be like in a work role. Ask a colleague with a reputation for being a skilled interviewer, or a peer you respect, to sit in on the applicant's next interview to double-check your hunch and to ensure you're not simply reacting to a personal bias or prejudice.

Success on the "Customer Service Stage" takes a great cast, a super script, great support, and great direction. Never compromise on casting, and never sacrifice rigor in the selection process to a desire to trim hiring costs or fill open jobs faster. Putting the right people in the right roles is critical to everything else in the production.

> You start with good people; you train and motivate them; you give them an opportunity to advance, then the organization succeeds.
>
> —J. W. "Bill" Marriott, Jr.
>   Chairman and CEO, Marriott Corporation

2

Keeping Your Best and Brightest

Revolve your world around the customer and more customers will revolve around you.

—Heather Williams

The connection between retaining your best service performers and creating happy customers is powerful and cuts across virtually every dividing line: industry, size of company, scale of market, you name it. It's not difficult to see why.

- Customers want and value reliability, ease, efficiency, and consistency in their service experiences with you—with the appropriate dose of friendliness and caring. From the *customer* standpoint, dealing with experienced people is basic to building not just a relationship, but a true partnership.

- Experience is still the best teacher. No Web-based training module or classroom session can hope to replicate the database that resides squarely between your employees' ears, the tacit knowledge that can only be gained by working on the front lines week after week, year after year, dealing with every customer question, demand, or complaint under the sun. Your true "personnel cost" is much more than a salary total. It's every dime, every minute, and every ounce of energy anyone in your organization has spent recruiting, interviewing, hiring, training, supervising, coaching, and profiting from your people.

It's not just common sense that tells us there's a strong correlation between employee retention and organizational performance—a number of studies bear it out. In his book *The Loyalty Effect: The Hidden Force Behind Growth, Profits and Lasting Value,* author Fred Reichheld, director emeritus at Bain and Company, reports that when one organization examined the connection in its stores between employee loyalty and productivity, it found that the top third in employee retention were also in the top third in productivity, and their sales were also 22 percent higher than stores ranked in the bottom third of retention. A study of fast-food chains in Reichheld's book found that outlets with low staff turnover had profit margins that were more than 50 percent higher than stores with high turnover.

We're not suggesting your goal should be to create lifetime service employees. The reality is that many customer service positions are still looked upon as stepping stones to bigger things. The more prudent stance, retention experts say, is to identify the "tipping point" for your frontline staff—the length of employment where turnover most often occurs—and to pull out the stops to convince your top performers—those who are most competent, caring, and resilient—to stay with you beyond that juncture.

Employees who are only with you in body and not in spirit, on the other hand, can do more harm to your company's reputation for service quality by staying than by leaving. If repeated attempts to help elevate their performance or change their attitudes fall short, they should be encouraged to look for new opportunities elsewhere in the company or be let go. As the adage goes, "*Change* the people or change the *people*!"

Customers Are Watching

Just as your style of service determines whether you'll retain a customer, your style of managing is basic to the retention and service achievements of your people. Yet we all know that there are managers who still use their authority as a club to beat the drive, the sense of fun, and the risk taking out of people.

Not only does this have a profound effect on the people we manage, it also has an impact—typically more direct than we give it credit for—on customers. If you've ever stood at a checkout counter, held captive by a supervisor who deems it more important to chastise a clerk about yesterday's pricing error than to ensure you get prompt service, you've seen the downside of poor service management in action.

In several landmark studies, service researchers Benjamin Schneider and David Bowen have shown that *customer service satisfaction* is directly related to *employee job satisfaction*. Their work, done both jointly and independently over a ten-year period, points to a number of specific ways that job satisfaction is tied to customer satisfaction:

1. Customers "see into" the organization through a unique window: the actions and words of frontline employees. They assume the attitude and treatment they experience at the front line of an organization is an accurate representation of the way the organization wants customers to be treated.

2. The treatment that customers experience directly reflects the treatment employees receive from their managers. The "kick-the-cat" phenomenon is real. If you're at the front line and your boss shows you little respect, fails to listen, or gives you a hard time, you pass that treatment on—sometimes to other employees, sometimes to family, and sometimes to customers.

3. On the whole, employees desire to give good service and receive customer accolades for it. When conditions prevent or prohibit employees from doing what they believe to be in the best interests of the customer—when company policies are overly restrictive or managers refuse to even consider viewing situations through the customer's eyes—they become defensive and prickly.

On the positive side, Schneider and Bowen have found in their work that employees and customers both rate service quality highest in branches of an organization where (1) there is an enthusiastic service emphasis, (2) managers emphasize the importance of service to unit success, (3) there is an active effort to retain all accounts, not just "high net" customers, (4) the number of well-trained frontline people at the unit is sufficient to provide customers good service, (5) technology is well-maintained and supplies are plentiful, and (6) employees believe they have a reasonable opportunity for career advancement in the organization.[6]

Only when the economics of the workplace are such that there are few jobs and a lot of people wanting them will people put up with anything just for a paycheck. But as soon as conditions improve, the ones with gumption, initiative, and talent—the ones you really want to keep because they're the hardest to find and replace—will be gone. The question you have to answer is whether you want to depend on crisis conditions for employee retention or look for a better way.

Top Ways to Retain

As a manager, you have a variety of weapons in your arsenal to keep your employees coming back:

• *Good Management Trumps All.* Survey after survey shows that people don't leave organizations; they leave bosses. Research from Talent Keepers, a Florida consulting firm, found that while employees are attracted to organizations for factors such as pay, benefits, reputation, or the nature of the job itself, within short order it's the quality of their relationship with managers that matters most. If front liners are respected, listened to, provided good working environments, and recognized for their hard work—and if managers routinely keep their promises and take responsibility for company policies—it often holds more value in employees' eyes than promotional opportunities, compensation, or health benefits (unless they are paid well below market averages). Conversely, when people are treated like interchangeable parts or simply "butts in seats," managers will usually be rewarded with a marginally productive, listless, and resentful workforce that will leap at the first new job opportunity that promises they'll be treated more like sentient life forms.

• *Compensation and Benefits.* While money may not be everything, it's a very close second to whatever's first. Service-distinctive organizations not uncommonly pay above the average for their industry, using the tactic (1) to attract good people and (2) to keep top talent from seeking greener pastures. FedEx package sorters start out at about double the minimum wage, and even part-timers are eligible for bonuses and profit sharing. Costco warehouse stores pay their full-time hourly workers significantly more than rivals like Sam's Club, the Wal-Mart subsidiary, believing it will result in reduced turnover and greater productivity. A study by *Business Week* bears Costco's thinking out. The magazine crunched the numbers of both Costco and Sam's Club and found that "by compensating employees generously to motivate and retain good workers—one-fifth of who are unionized—Costco gets lower turnover and higher productivity." Costco's labor costs also proved lower than Wal-Mart's as a percentage of sales, and its hourly workers in the United States sell more per square foot. On the turnover front, the *Business Week* study found that only 6 percent of Costco employees left after their first year on the job, compared with 21 percent at Sam's Club.[7]

Other service-focused companies use attractive benefit packages, including company-paid health care, to lure and retain the part-time workers that are essential to executing their service strategies. Seattle-based Starbucks was among the first organizations to offer health benefits to part-timers. Timberland offers employees such unique benefits as a $3,000 subsidy for a hybrid car and forty hours of paid volunteer work per year. Quicken Loans provides company-sponsored bus rides to Cleveland Cavaliers games, a team owned by Quicken's chief executive officer (CEO).

• *Special Treatment.* In lieu of money, respect for individual concerns can compensate in a variety of ways. Instead of forcing everyone to fit into the same employee box, recognize that people each need and value different things. For parents with young children, for example, it may be flexibility around day care, and for those whose children are a little older, it may be the opportunity to attend an occasional school program in the middle of the afternoon. For employees with aging or infirm parents, flexing work schedules so they can provide much needed care or transportation can prove a big benefit. Ditto for opportunities to telecommute or occasionally work out of a home office. At First Bank and Trust in Lubbock, Texas, CEO Barry Orr encourages employees to "not miss that special ballgame with Junior or Mom's and Muffins or a dental appointment." Employees are asked to simply make up the needed time off by working later or on the weekend. No one monitors it; the honor system is sufficient to ensure bank employees repay time off for special events with time on the job.

• *Special Contracts and Perks.* Tie specific types of performance achievements to specific payoffs, whether they be monetary or symbolic. A "piece of the action"—the increased revenue from a formerly static account that's now growing, or the savings from a suggestion—tells your people you value their efforts. Similarly, tickets to athletic or cultural events, enhanced discounts on the company's products and services, and other "spiffs" keep them from feeling taken for granted.

• *Training.* For today's knowledgeable workers, one of the most enlivening and enriching experiences is training that helps them do their jobs better. They know performance counts and that, in many cases, they're being judged on how well their customers say they're serving. Developing new talents or getting a refresher on old ones helps them stay on top of their game. It also communicates the organization's continuing commitment to them. Research from the "Emerging Work Force Study" reviewed in a *Business Week* article reported that 35 percent of employees who don't receive regular training plan to look for another job within twelve months.[8]

• *Cross-Training.* The more hats your people can wear, the more valuable they can be to the organization. If their current specialty goes away or is de-emphasized, they know and you know that they're ready and able to fill an emerging need instead of filling out an application for unemployment insurance. What's more, having people pretrained for other jobs helps you meet unexpected demands, from the need to replace someone who departs unexpectedly, to coping with the occasional (and unpredictable) overload situation, to the ability to respond quickly to new demands and opportunities. People also appreciate the change of pace provided by doing other jobs or tasks, even for short periods.

• *Lateral Job Movement.* The most exciting and fulfilling job becomes stagnant and predictable over time. At many best-of-breed service companies, lateral "developmental assignments" are used to challenge, reward, and motivate people who can't move up (because so many layers of "up" have been eliminated in recent years). Giving your people the opportunity to move laterally not only gives them a chance to rise to a new challenge, but also helps them gain a new perspective on what they've been doing.

• *Empowerment.* According to Richard Leider, author of *The Power of Purpose,* one of the biggest problems today isn't burnout, it's rustout. So many people in our organizations are capable of doing so much more than we've ever asked (or allowed) them to do. So let 'em. The more ownership they assume for the responsibilities built into their job, the more likely they are to stay with it, no matter (and perhaps because of) how challenging they find it.

• *Reward and Recognition.* What gets rewarded gets repeated. If you want people to stay and grow with you, recognize and reward them, not just for their years of service but for their accomplishments along the way. For most people, the research shows that being thanked for a job well done is a more powerful motivator than money. It says you're paying attention to their individual (or team) performance and that you recognize how hard they're working, how much they're contributing, how emotionally taxing it can be to deal with customers each and every day, and how valuable they are.

> We have a belief that our guests will only receive the kind of treatment we want them to receive if the cast members receive that same kind of treatment from their managers.
>
> —Walt Disney World Handbook

Imperative 2

Know Your Customers Intimately

You subscribe to all the trade journals. You bookmark the best blog sites. You do an annual survey of your customers. The company even has done some market research and a few focus groups. You sit next to the people on the phones from time to time. You regularly talk with the salespeople to learn what they are hearing from their customers, prospects, and suspects. You even jump in and work with tough customer problems when asked.

You *are* close to the customer—right? Perhaps. And then again, perhaps not.

Knowing your customer intimately means more than having a passing acquaintance with the market research of your industry or company. It means spending time listening, understanding, and responding—often in unique and creative ways—to your customers' evolving needs and shifting expectations. Knowing your customer intimately means that people at *all* levels of the organization find time to gain insights by meeting with, listening to, and learning from customers in highly focused ways. Knowing your customer intimately means knowing each other's business so well that you can anticipate each other's problems and opportunities—and can work on solutions and strategies together.

3

Why Customer Satisfaction Isn't Enough

Customers perceive service in their own unique, idiosyncratic, emotional, irrational and totally human terms. Perception is all there is.

—Tom Peters
Management Consultant

For as long as we can remember the promised land of service-focused organizations—the accomplishment that, once achieved, suggested they'd arrived among the ranks of customer service exemplars—has been represented by two sought after words: *customer satisfaction*. When customers report being "very satisfied" or "satisfied" on our surveys, we take it as a sign of their continued loyalty, believing they'll continue to spend their dollars with us and recommend us to others. Yet the truth is that while satisfying customers beats the alternative, it is rarely enough to produce the kind of devoted clientele that will stay committed to your company in the face of new price-slashing competitors, the periodic hiccup in product or service quality, or other threats to their continued patronage. Consider what the word *satisfaction* really connotes. Webster's defines it as "good enough to fulfill a need or requirement," and common synonyms are "sufficient" and "adequate." Hardly the stuff of inspiration and devotion.

As service quality researchers have discovered in recent years, measures of satisfaction are often poor predictors of the most important yardstick of any service effort: Will customers not only come back for more, but also go out of their way to recommend you to others?

Love That Customer

Consider the perspective of Robert A. "Bob" Peterson, who holds the John T. Stuart III Centennial Chair in Business Administration at the University of Texas, Austin. His opinion, based on his own research, is that "love that customer" is pretty powerful stuff.

For years, Peterson was troubled that so many people were talking about the joys of customer satisfaction, but his research wasn't showing a very strong connection between satisfaction and retention—repeat business. He found that in most surveys of customer satisfaction, something around 85 percent of an organization's customers claimed to be "satisfied" with the service they received but still showed a willingness to wander away to other providers if the mood or the price or the color of the advertising banner were right.

Peterson believes that we have undervalued the emotional aspects of customer service and that there is a highly personal, subjective agenda that we both fail to ask about in customer research and fail to deal with in-service delivery. Only by adding words like *love* and *hate* to our surveys and having the audacity to stand up to the need to incorporate much stronger feelings than *like* and *satisfaction* in our objectives can we get a handle on this crucial component of customer loyalty. And the only way to get to the heart of the matter is by getting our information straight from customers—from their own selfish (and sometimes flawed) perspectives, based on their own experiences, and expressed in their own words.

The payoff is the kind of in-depth understanding that can help nurture a truly productive relationship—or save one from going bad. Peterson believes that customers with strong feelings about the organization are the most predictable customers. "Customers who feel strongly about your organization—positively or negatively—are the customers *most likely* and *least likely* to do business with you again," he says.

Recent research by the Gallup Organization corroborates and builds on many of Peterson's findings. In a *Harvard Business Review* article titled, "Managing Your Human Sigma,"[9] John H. Fleming, Curt Coffman, and James K. Harter of Gallup examined the nature of employee interactions with customers and found that emotions had a significantly larger effect on both parties' judgments and behavior than rational thinking did.

The Gallup team found that customers who rate themselves as "extremely satisfied" on surveys fall into two distinct categories: those who have a strong emotional connection to the company and those who do not. In a multiyear study of hundreds of companies and millions of customers and employees, Gallup found that:

• "Emotionally satisfied" customers contribute far more to the bottom line than "rationally satisfied" customers do, even though the latter rate themselves as equally "satisfied" on customer surveys.

• Surprisingly, the behavior of rationally *satisfied* customers looked no different from that of *dissatisfied* customers. For a large U.S. bank in the study, the attrition rate of dissatisfied customers was on par with that of rationally satisfied customers, or those who described themselves as extremely satisfied but scored low on an "emotional attachment" metric that measured four dimensions: confidence (Does the company deliver on its promises?), integrity (Am I treated the way I deserve to be treated?), pride (a sense of positive identification with the company), and passion (Is the company irreplaceable in my life and a perfect fit for me?). The attrition rate of bank customers who were emotionally satisfied, on the other hand, was on average 37 percent lower.

• For all types of companies in the research, Gallup found that emotionally engaged customers delivered a 23 percent premium over the average customer in terms of profitability, revenue, and relationship growth.

Measuring via Customer-Derived Language

Does this mean you should start sprinkling words like "love," "enchanted," "awful," or "hideous" on your customer surveys? What about the implications for organizations with lesser aspirations, where in their minds moving the needle from *"somewhat satisfied"* to *"satisfied"* might represent a quantum leap in service quality? Is it even realistic to think you can evoke customer passion or love when you're selling more pedestrian products or services, such as those that meet basic needs but do little to excite or inspire?

How customer expectations change based on the nature of business transactions can provide some guidance on the language you opt to use on surveys. Consider what customers experience when they purchase an everyday household product versus when they engage in a more emotion-laden service experience. We buy many of the products we do to meet basic needs. In purchasing a new refrigerator, trash compactor, or bed, for example, we usually want to fulfill simple requirements—to keep food cold, to dispose of trash, or to facilitate comfortable sleep. To be sure, there are some purchases—a Harley-Davidson motorcycle, an Apple iPad, or women's Manolo Blahnik shoes come to mind—that create an emotional bond and may border for some on a religious experience, although such products are in the minority.

Now think about a service experience like a night at a five-star restaurant, a guided whitewater rafting trip, or even your own honeymoon. Recalling your fondest memories of the experience, it's unlikely that the highest measure on most surveys—"completely satisfied"—could truly capture your feelings about the experience.

What separates most service experiences from product purchasing scenarios—and what should act as a guide for how you craft surveys to gauge customers' repurchase intentions—is that the service is performed or occurs in a way that physically involves the customer. Imagine that a customer who needed a trash compactor showed up at the factory to help the manufacturer produce the compactor that the customer ultimately planned to purchase. Sound ludicrous? This is how service happens every time.

For example, if a customer gives a "completely satisfied" rating to his five-star restaurant experience, managers of that restaurant are likely to view that as a service and word-of-mouth marketing coup. But if applied to the emotional yardstick we've described throughout this chapter, it might truly only be a "C" grade in that customer's eyes, meaning the restaurant fulfilled base requirements but barely passed muster. This explains why—as the Peterson and Gallup research confirms—the majority of customers who leave one organization to go to a competitor say, when asked, that they were "satisfied or completely satisfied" with the organization they just left behind.

Shifting from a satisfaction paradigm to one that more closely matches how humans judge a service experience is only part of the solution. The need for reliability in market research techniques can't be sacrificed even if the thing you are evaluating is more subjective. Trusting one customer's definition of "awesome" to be comparable to another's, for example, is questionable science.

The key to improving the measurement process to get a more accurate reading of how service experiences impact loyalty is to seek out and use the language of the customer, not of the researcher. If "awesome" is the word that customers use to describe the service experience, then "awesome" it should be. Such customer-derived language will be inexact and slippery. But one way around that challenge might be to begin asking respondents to recall their very best service experience and use the word or phrase that best characterizes it. That word could then be used for the upper end of the scale for all other questions asked in phone or face-to-face interviews. Repeating the process for the lower end provides the same semantic differences in the customer's language. This methodology enables Customer A's "excellent" (his highest rating) to be reliably compared to Customer B's "outstanding" (her highest rating).[10]

Romancing the Customer

Even in traditional manufacturing (and manufacturing-style services), where "careful is correct and rational is right" has long been the managerial axiom, service quality is being recognized as the marketing edge that can differentiate one commodity offering from another. The service tide in which we've all been swept up makes it imperative that we pay increasing attention to whatever it takes, one-on-one and one-by-one, to earn the love and loyalty of our customers.

We don't have the luxury of putting off this transformation. Inspired by their years of experience, well-publicized product quality improvement efforts, and heightened service delivery rhetoric alike, customers are getting increasingly emotional, even passionate, about their service experiences. Listen to the raves of the L.L. Bean, JetBlue, Fairmont Hotels, Umpqua Bank, Publix Super Markets, and Zappos.com faithful and you'll hear more "love stories" than you'll find on the drugstore paperback rack. Listen, as well, to the tales of anger and woe told by disgruntled customers, and you'll find that novelist Stephen King doesn't have a corner on horror stories.

In this time of passion, how do you use the concept of "customer intimacy" to create long-term loyalty? Start by seeing customer transactions not as a random collection of single experiences, but as a relationship. Relationships in business, just as those in our personal lives, are built on knowledge, caring, and experience. Today, segmentation, personalization, and niche marketing are the name of the game in virtually every industry sector. Customers are no longer shapeless and featureless mass markets. They're specific, small groups with their own unique view of what constitutes quality service. What they want and how they want it—and how they do or don't get it—add up to an index of "customer love" that ultimately determines whether they'll ever come back and do business with you again.

It's an adjunct of the Rule of Psychological Reciprocity: If you don't show interest in your customers, they won't show interest in you. If you don't trust them, they won't trust you. And if you don't care passionately, sincerely, and constantly about not just meeting but exceeding their needs, they won't see you as being any better or any worse than any other organization they have done business with. They most certainly won't fall in love with your organization.

In short, "ya gotta love that customer" if you expect the customer to love you back.

> Most good innovation comes from customers. The more time we spend thinking in the ivory tower in San Jose, the worse off we're going to be.
>
> —John Donahue
> CEP, eBay

4

Listening Is a Contact Sport

Two ears, one mouth—do the math.

—author unknown

Listening well is a rarity in our society. That helps explain the popularity of psychologists, the scale of the divorce rate, and why there are so many self-help books with communications as their central theme. As a manager, you have to serve as both listening post and traffic analyst. Neither is as simple as it sounds.

Part of the challenge of listening is filtering out the noise of bias and defensiveness. When your frontline workers hear customers suggesting ways your business could do more for them, the instinctive response is to determine how much additional work that might mean. When service employees hear negative comments from customers about their or the organization's service performance, they have a natural tendency to defend and protect.

Their inherent sense of "possessiveness" about the delivery processes and their tendency to take complaints as a personal attack make it harder for people at the front line to listen in a nonjudgmental way. Although your people are up close and personal with customers on a day-to-day basis, as a manager you are in a better position to listen effectively. Being one step removed from the action, you should have less defensiveness and a broader perspective than the immediate moment.

Additionally, frontline workers typically listen to customers for cues on what to do in what order, instructions for tasks to be completed, or requests for problems to be solved. The "immediate action required" nature of this exchange makes it difficult to spot themes and trends at the front line. As a manager, you're more likely to have a forest-wide perspective than a tree-by-tree view.

Listen, Understand, Respond

Listening does not mean simply looking at someone while they talk—or adding the obligatory "uh-huhs" in the right spots during phone conversations—and then doing something in response. There's an important middle piece to the puzzle: Listening means actively seeking to understand another person. That's why we say it's a contact sport. Listening without contact, listening without a *dramatic connection*, is like looking without seeing. Given the uniqueness of really being heard, customers long remember those frontline workers who listen well.

Active listening is responding in a way that says, "I understand what you are saying"; dramatic listening is responding in a way that communicates, "I understand what you are saying *and* I value what you are trying to communicate." Whether focused on questions, complaints, or collecting new ideas, dramatic listening leaves customers with the rare feeling of being heard and confident that your organization will honor the information received and will take action where warranted.

Many organizations like to boast of their commitment to great customer listening, pointing to stacks of survey research to prove how serious they are about capturing the voice of the customer. Yet the reality is that today's customers—and the employees who serve them—too often feel oversurveyed and undervalued. They sense that companies are going through the motions in seeking their input, simply checking off the box marked "touched base with customers," then returning to business as usual and giving little consideration to their input. Many of these listening strategies seek facts but not feelings, conversation instead of candor. But only by having the courage to ask for unvarnished opinions from customers—and then listening without donning defensive armor—can you hope to get the kind of honest feedback that leads to meaningful service improvements.

It's also important to listen to the things your frontline people can tell you about constantly changing customer needs, expectations, issues, and concerns. In settings from Walt Disney World to the call centers of USAA Insurance, customer contact people debrief each other periodically to spot new problems or requests, emerging opportunities, and the influence of larger market conditions. When managers act on their information, the message comes through loud and clear: Pay attention to your customers. We're interested in what they're telling you. That's how we learn to serve them better.

Six Ways to Listen for Consumer Needs and Expectations

There are lots of ways to listen to your customers, and to do it well, you need to master and use more than one style. It's like using a belt and suspenders to hold up your pants. The redundant systems reinforce each other, but they do so in different styles with different strengths and weaknesses. Consider the following.

1. *Face-to-Face.* More and more managers are uncomfortable with the idea that the information they are getting is indirect. They want to know things directly and personally, to see and hear for themselves what customers are experiencing on the front lines. Such firsthand knowledge can provide the kind of insights—and make the kind of impact—that reading static customer evaluation reports never can.

One health care executive we know of makes a point of spending one day a week on the front lines of his hospital, often wearing a volunteer's anonymous coat to reduce the odds that people will slant what they're saying because they know who's listening. Interestingly, he says the customer he's listening to isn't just the patient. He listens to his people, too. His reasoning is simple: His personal customer isn't the patient; it's his people, because those people treat the patients, he doesn't.

Maxine Clark, founder and CEO of Build-a-Bear Workshop, the unique business that allows children to build their own stuffed animals, visits two to three of the franchises per week, chatting up customers and touching base with employees. Clark says a key to her success as a leader is "never forgetting what it's like to be a customer" of the store.[11]

Front liners and managers can learn a lot about the customer experience simply by being more observant. One hotel chain instituted a "follow me" program that had front desk clerks ask repeat guests if they would, for a discounted rate, allow the bell man to unobtrusively hang around and "watch you unpack and settle in."

The program proved a major source of learning about the small, irritating "workarounds" that hotel customers faced, such as having to place the suitcase of a traveling companion on the floor because the hotel only provided one luggage rack, having to unplug and find a place for hotel-provided hair dryers when guests bring their own, and much more. By "listening with their eyes," hotel employees found ways to enhance the customer experience that guests may never have suggested on comment cards.

2. *Layered Group Listening.* How many times have you had a frontline employee tell you, "I wish you could have heard this complaint? We've been getting it a lot, and I think it's something we really need to fix." Layered group listening is a variation on the focus group technique that enables layers of the organization to listen to customers at the same time. In Figure 4-1, the X's represent customers, the O's are frontline employees, and the □'s are supervisors and managers.

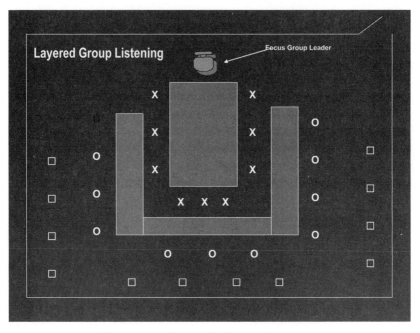

Figure 4-1. Layered Group Listening.

The listening process can be done in three rounds, each lasting forty-five to sixty minutes. In round one, the customers are interviewed by a focus group leader (⊗). Front liners (O's) can only ask questions for clarification—they cannot explain or defend—and managers (□'s) cannot say anything—they only get to listen. After the first round, customers leave, the O's move to the center table, and □'s move to where O's had been, and the second round occurs—front liners react to what they heard from customers, and managers only ask questions for clarification.

In round three, front liners and managers spend a round problem-solving based on what they learned together. Some organizations also find it valuable to bring customers back to participate in this third round.

The upshot is managers get a firsthand understanding of the frustrations, concerns, and plaudits that frontline employees

hear customers voice every day. Sometimes it takes such exposure—hearing straight from the horse's mouth—for managers to
truly grasp how service problems are affecting customers' willingness to keep doing business with a company. On the flip side,
it's also heartening to hear kudos about the positive things your
staff has done to win customers' loyalty or make them sing your
firm's praises to others.

3. *Comment and Complaint Analysis.* Some customers will
tell you what's on their mind face to face. Some won't risk the
chance of confrontation or embarrassment, but will fill out simple "Tell Us, Rate Us, Help Us" comment cards. Tracking them
can give you a continuing barometric reading on how you're
doing. More extensive contacts, such as complaint and compliment letters, can be mined for detailed insights into past experiences and future preferences. Keep in mind these work best
when customers perceive their comments make a difference.

4. *Multichannel Response Systems.* Make it easy to listen
by making it easy for customers to contact you through toll-
free numbers, e-mail, Web-based text chat, Facebook, Twitter,
and more. Most service-focused companies today have Web-
enabled call centers that route, queue, and prioritize incoming
e-mail from customers, enabling customer service reps to handle e-mail and real-time Web requests as efficiently as calls to
toll-free numbers.

Don't make trying to find a toll-free number on your website like a game of "Where's Waldo?" Plenty of customers have
a good reason for wanting to contact you via phone or Web
chat versus sending e-mail or visiting your frequently asked
questions (FAQ) page; either they can't find answers to their
questions using those resources, or they need more detailed
and nuanced responses than those avenues provide. List your
toll-free number boldly on every Web page.

5. *Monitor the Online Buzz.* More companies are listening
to their customers by monitoring online discussion boards,
tweets, chat rooms, and blogs to stay on top of what's being
said about their products or services. While they know they
can't control online word of mouth, and many of the rants may
be unfounded, they nonetheless see it as a valuable market

research tool. If companies come across a critical mass of complaints about some aspect of their performance, it may be a sign they need to follow up. Monitoring online commentary also can be a useful way of picking up new ideas for improving service, since offering such suggestions is one of the favorite pastimes of bloggers and users of online discussions boards. Remember, online communications should be a learning conversation, not a sales arena. And, with the growing popularity of Twitter, responding to tweets has become an essential part of communications. Often, customer complaints can be resolved on the spot, and delight occurs almost instantaneously.

6. *Customer Advisory Panels.* Your best customers, the ones who have been with you for years, represent not only a valued relationship but also a source of savvy insight into your service operations. Use them like a board of directors for the front line. Your worst customers can also be an asset when you find active ways to listen. Emerald People's Utility District (EPUD), a small public power co-op based in Eugene, Oregon, gets customers involved in various committees and study groups. Arizona Public Service (APS), a much larger regional utility and subsidiary of Pinnacle West based in Phoenix, has recruited some of the public interest advocates who once dogged its every step to bring their interest and energy inside the walls, where they can be applied in useful ways. Retailers have been known to use panels of customers to help them anticipate fashion trends, and electronics companies often tap knowledgeable customers for feedback on design, standards, and pricing of their products.

The Power of Formal Research

Last, but certainly not least, there's the spectrum of more formal techniques for data collection. Mail-in, Web-based, and live surveys; focus groups; telemarketing contacts; mystery shopping services; demographic analysis; and random sampling of target audiences all help shade in the various colors of the big picture.

1. *Customer Surveys.* Face-to-face, via e-mail or snail mail, on websites, or over the telephone (or through a combination), ask customers to rate you on overall "delight" on the success of the last transaction they had with you, on specific aspects of your service delivery processes, and perhaps most important, on how likely they'd be to recommend you to colleagues or friends as well as whether they have recommended you. The latter two questions measure how well you've done at creating "passionate advocates" of your company. Then feed the results back into your organization. Be sure to make questions sound more like they are coming from a neighbor than a doctoral student!

Pay close attention to what your most loyal customers tell you is important. This helps determine what drives loyalty. For example, if you ask customers of an airline the most important feature as a passenger, safety will always top the list. But, if you examine what feature causes customers to pick one airline over another, safety will not likely be in the top five. It is important to know what is important to customers; it is also important to know what drives their loyalty. Be sure to ask both importance and performance questions. Measuring the two dimensions helps you avoid spending dollars on fixing things—or adding amenities—that have little impact on customer loyalty.

2. *Focus Groups.* Bringing current customers together to discuss the good, the bad, and the ugly of what you do puts flesh on the bones of survey data. Customers can problem-solve with you, rate and rank the relative importance of different aspects of your service (the moments of truth that define the shape and style of your services in customers' eyes), and explain how different elements of a transaction affect their perceptions of you. Employee focus groups work as well as customer focus groups. Bring a group of employees together and ask such questions as "What are our customers saying to you?" and "What gets in your way of delivering good service?" and "What can we do to help keep you fresh and renewed so you can better handle the challenge of dealing with customers all day?" Remember that focus groups can be virtual online, not just face to face.

3. *Employee Visit Teams.* Send teams of frontline workers, supervisors, and support people out to look at the customers' "points of contact" (with you as well as your competitors) from the customers' point of view. Their assignment is to bring back ideas for improving transactional quality based on customer experiences. What are the pluses and minuses of your service delivery processes viewed through the customer's eyes?

4. *Mystery Shopping Services.* Some companies specialize in playing the role of customer and giving feedback on your customer contact performance. The best ones work with you to develop checklists or evaluation scales based on your service vision statement; some will even put their people through your service training so they know exactly how your people are supposed to be doing things. As a twist, you can use your own employees as shoppers as well. It is also possible to do comparison shopping of your competition using your own criteria for good service.

5. *Toll-Free Hotlines and "Voice of the Customer" (VOC) Websites.* A good service recovery system almost always has a hotline or VOC website of some sort, with service employees trained and focused on resolving customer problems on first contact. Many customer-centric companies create toll-free lines or Web chats for specific product or service offerings, and others have gone multilingual. FedEx, for example, has an interactive voice response system that allows customers to speak to either English or Spanish customer service personnel. Customers who call in to register a complaint, make a suggestion, ask a question, or have a problem solved offer extremely valuable input on your service delivery system.

The key to making toll-free numbers and VOC websites work is data capture and analysis. It is more difficult than it sounds to get people in Department A to work with people in Department B on service process improvement. This is especially true when one of the departments is seen as the "complaint handling specialists." Incentives are usually needed. And objectives. And attention to detail.

6. *Benchmarking.* Started as a way to compare operational efficiencies with companies that have similar problems or challenges but aren't in your business (so data can be shared without concern for competitive consequences), benchmarking has become more broadly defined today as a way of looking for breakthrough ideas by seeing how others are seeing their customers. The original purpose of benchmarking related directly to improving service delivery processes by comparing operational ideas and numbers with a world-class company in another industry. That is still the best use possible, but don't overlook the teaching examples provided by any organization's comparative experiences.

> Listening is useless unless it creates actions which
> realign efforts based on what is learned.
>
> —Fred Smith
> Founder and Chairman,
> FedEx

5

A Complaining Customer Is Your Best Friend

One of the surest signs of a bad or declining relationship with a customer is the absence of complaints. Nobody is ever that satisfied, especially not over an extended period of time. The customer is either not being candid or not being contacted.

—Theodore Levitt
Business School Professor, Harvard University

As a manager, it can be easy to subscribe to "no news is good news" thinking when it comes to your staff's service performance. You work diligently to ensure your people have the right training, coaching, and technology to give customers their best every day, and you see firsthand much of the good work they do to solve vexing problems and address tough questions. When customer evaluation reports turn up only a handful of formal complaints, its natural—and comforting—to believe those numbers reflect the bang-up job your staff has done at creating a critical mass of happy customers.

But experts at TARP Worldwide, an Arlington, Virginia-based customer service research firm, will tell you it's also the kind of thinking that can prove dangerous to the health of your organization's bottom line. Too often, what these upset customers do instead of contacting the offending company is silently slip away to the competition, never to donate to your corporate coffers again. The truth is that most unhappy customers would rather switch than fight, usually because they don't like confrontation or are convinced their complaints will result in little substantive change.

The Trouble with Customer Silence

When it comes to customer relationships, silence isn't golden. The reality is that things often go wrong over the course of a service relationship, and when they do, you want to know about it, and the sooner the better. At least, you do if you're sincerely interested in building a long-term relationship that's strong enough to weather the occasional goof or glitch. Too often we encounter managers who, when presented with bad news, revert to playground behaviors and hum loudly or cover their ears to avoid having to hear it.

Just as personal relationships have their occasional rough spots, so too will a customer relationship have its ups and downs. If there's real long-term value in the relationship, both parties will have an incentive to overcome the periodic problems and, through the process of doing so, make the relationship even stronger. In contrast, an absence of candor that causes one partner to gloss over or fail to mention problems reflects declining trust and a deteriorating relationship.

A strong, enduring customer service relationship will be founded on clear, open communications—whether the matter at hand is good or bad. Customers who take the time to bring their problems to us or offer advice on how we can better meet their needs are customers who believe we care enough to act on their complaints, not just feel good about their compliments. They're telling us they still see value in the relationship continuing—if, that is, things can get back to a sound and mutually satisfying level.

Wise companies view customer complaints as the pearl inside the oyster. The fact is that customers who complain can become even *more* loyal to your company than those who experience no problems with you at all . . . if their complaints are handled in an effective and rapid manner. Research by Marriott Hotels, for example, found that for customers who had experienced some problems during their stay but had those issues satisfactorily resolved before they left the hotel, 94 percent said they would use the hotel again. On the other hand, 89 percent of customers who had experienced *no* problems during their stay said they intended to come back to the Marriott again.

By contrast, avoiding complaints, pretending that everything is "just peachy" (even when you know it isn't), and pretending to assertively solicit customer feedback with one hand while backhanding the customer for daring to utter a discouraging word with the other are sure signs that the relationship has not achieved enough maturity to weather the candor. That way lies dissolution. And, since in the event of divorce, a valued customer always gets custody of the "business" they bring to a relationship, you'll not only have to replace them, but you'll also have to watch them take up with your bitterest rivals: your competition.

Stimulating Complaints

While it might be counterintuitive to think that people who've been wronged—seriously or otherwise—would hesitate to complain about the perceived injustice, research sheds light on why customers often choose "flight over fight."

Consider, for example, why an upset diner usually answers "fine" if asked how everything was, when, in fact, the meal and/or the service were a disappointment. Or consider why customers often wear clothes and shoes that are half a size too large or too small rather than return them to the store for a replacement that fits better. Don't these customers know how much we want and need their feedback today?

In point of fact, they don't know. There are three basic reasons why customers choose to vote with their feet and go looking for another service provider rather than stick around and try to work the problem through with us:

1. They don't think we care.
2. They don't have any hope for a satisfactory resolution to their problem—they don't think anything good is going to happen, even if we do care.
3. They don't have any courage—experience has taught them that "no good turn goes unpunished," leading them to fear that the service provider will find a way to retaliate against them the next time.

However, customers are getting more and more vocal. Some research shows that of the almost 60 percent of customers who had a bad experience in the last year, 66 percent told someone at the company and 80 percent told a friend or colleague.[12] The silent majority is getting less and less silent. When the pocketbook gets squeezed, customers are more vocal about letting someone know when they do not get value. Customers at the end of the 2008 to 2010 recession were 14 percent more likely to complain than before the recession.[13]

In another study, 79 percent of customers who had a negative experience told others about it, according to the "Customer Experience Report North America 2010" from RightNow.com and Harris Interactive. Eighty-five percent of customers wanted to warn others about the pitfalls of doing business with that company, and 66 percent wanted to discourage others from buying from that company. In addition, 76 percent indicated that word of mouth influenced their purchasing decisions.[14]

In addition to saying something, customers have another tactic when they have a bad experience—they leave! Convergys reports that 44 percent of customers stop doing business with a company immediately, and another 15 percent exit as soon as their contract is up![15] Other researchers found that 82 percent of consumers quit doing business with a company because of a bad customer experience, up from 59 percent four years ago.[16] Think about that. Over half of customers who have had a bad experience go elsewhere.

Today, social media carries five times the impact of traditional word of mouth. And beware of the viral effect. Over 60 percent of customers who hear about a bad experience on social media stop doing business with or avoid doing business with the offending company.[17] This "secondary smoke" phenomenon will grow as the use of social media increases and more and more consumers are digital natives, not digital immigrants.

Warts and All

Over the years, businesses have done a pretty fair job of convincing customers to suffer in silence. Now, when we want this kind of informed feedback, we have to literally coax customers to provide it. There are a lot of reasons for this state of affairs:

- In some cases, we've lulled ourselves into thinking no news is good news, or that it's better to "let sleeping dogs lie."
- Sometimes we fear that if we seek and receive customer complaints and no corrective action ensues, we might be perceived in a worse light than if we'd left well enough alone. Research, however, contradicts that assumption: *Better to have asked and not acted, it finds, than not to have asked at all.*
- In some cases, we simply haven't figured out how to effectively ask for complaints without sounding almost masochistic: "Please, tell us how bad we are."
- When customers do take the time to complain, but jaded or indifferent frontline employees discount the complaint by saying "we hear a lot of that" or "that tends to happen quite a bit here toward the end of the quarter," customers feel their complaints aren't taken seriously and are hesitant to speak up again. If it happens enough, they'll simply pull up stakes for greener pastures.

How to Make Complaining Easier

Complaining customers are important in and of themselves. Their relationship with us is in obvious jeopardy and needs to be returned to a positive state. Complaining customers also are important because, statistically speaking, they represent other dissatisfied customers who are convinced that there's no point in telling us about their bad experiences with us. These customers are saying, "Please don't throw us away. We want the opportunity to be your customer again." The following are some tactics to help you get the most from those encounters.

1. *When you have an opportunity to address a complainant face to face, listen.* Work consciously at graciousness and control. Avoid becoming defensive or acting stern, cold, or judgmental. Especially avoid attempting to explain why the problem occurred. When they are levying complaints, customers are not particularly interested in your explanations for poor service, let alone what *they* should have done differently. They want to know (1) that they are being heard, and (2) that their comments are valued. Your explanations of why things work the way they do ("I'm just stating our policy") will be seen as defensive and will only aggravate and irritate.

2. *Treat complaints about your customer contact people as an opportunity.* Use the complaints for problem-solving and learning, not for rebuke and judgment. If you punish your frontline people when they bring you customer complaints or feedback, they will find ways to keep future feedback from you. *Keep in mind that the customer is not always right.* Research shows that about 30 percent of all service problems are actually caused by the customer; they fail to read user manuals or other important literature they're sent, plead ignorance about refund policies, ask you to share proprietary information about competitors, or simply make unreasonable requests. The objective isn't to assign blame and hand out punishment. It's to find out what happened, why, what you can do to resolve it this time, and what you can do to prevent it from happening again.

3. *Be assertive in soliciting customer feedback.* Nothing you or your people are doing is more important than taking care of customers. That process doesn't end with ringing up a sale. Stimulate the dialogue with statements like, "We are really anxious to do all we can to improve our service, and your feedback would be very helpful." Don't shut the door on additional details, either. When they've gotten through the key points of the story, probe for helpful details and other ideas: "Thanks, that helps a lot. What else could we do to improve our service?"

4. *Encourage your frontline people to ask for feedback.* Make it clear by words and actions that you think customers can help you build rewarding, long-term, and profitable relationships that benefit everyone involved. Be a good role model by asking customers for feedback in the presence of your frontline staff. Listen, understand, and respond to what your staffers have been hearing so they know that you'll act on what they can tell you.

5. *Use negative feedback to improve performance, not punish people.* When you get complaints from customers regarding your people, thank the customer involved for the information and make it clear that you will check into the problem, but without either scapegoating your employees or "shooting the messenger" by defending your people on general principles. Then, when you meet with your frontline person, present the feedback, not in a blaming or judgmental way, but with a descriptive "Let's figure out what we can do to resolve this situation" type of approach.

6. *Be sure to circle back to customers to let them know what you did.* Recent research showed that while 95 percent of firms surveyed indicate they collect customer information, only 10 percent actually "deploy" a change or policy based on customer feedback, and only 5 percent of firms tell customers that they used their feedback.[18] Another research study found that 88 percent of customers are less likely to buy from companies who leave complaints on social media unanswered!

7. *Don't take sides.* If you find yourself in the line of fire between the customer and your employee, take the high

ground. Instead of choosing sides, your best approach will be to try to collect facts and make a decision based on the *performance*, not the *people* involved. Remember that win/lose situations leave losers (and negative feelings) in their aftermath. Your goal should be to strike a balance between reaffirming the customer for complaining and reinforcing your people so they'll continue to have the confidence to deal with customers.

> Your most unhappy customers are your greatest source of learning.
>
> —Bill Gates

6

Little Things
Mean a Lot

It's not the one thousand dollar things that upset the customer, but the five buck things that bug them.

—Earl Fletcher
Sales and Management Trainer,
Volkswagen Canada

New arrivals to the combat zones of Vietnam quickly learned that the difference between a veteran and a novice was far more than war stories. They had an expression for it on the front lines: "grunt eyes." Grunts were the enlisted ranks of the infantry—low rank, little prestige, people whose job description started and ended with the simple requirement, "Do what the 'old man' tells you to do."

Those with grunt eyes were able to see things a new in-country recruit would completely miss. And there was little correlation with rank. Whether you were a captain or a private, you only acquired grunt eyes in the field, paying attention to every sight, sound, smell, impulse, clue, and condition that often could make the difference between life and death. It was something learned, not something taught. The common skeptic's question, immortalized in the movie *Full Metal Jacket,* was "I see you talk the talk, but do you walk the walk?"

As a manager, you've no doubt learned a fair amount of service talk in recent years. But have you also learned the service walk? Have you developed grunt eyes attuned to your own frontline conditions? Do you really notice and understand the subtleties of what you see? The survival of your business is riding on it. According to our survey research, about 22 percent of the difference between passionate and dispassionate customers can be accounted for by an organization's ability to recognize and manage the details that really matter for customers.

Attention to details is a prime characteristic of Knock Your Socks Off Service.

Fred Smith, founder and chairman of FedEx, begins many of his visits to various cities by hopping into a FedEx delivery van and riding with a driver to see his operations where they most affect the customer. Bill Marriott, chairman of the hotel chain that bears the family name, often takes a turn at the front desk checking in guests. If he sees a dirty ashtray in the lobby, he empties it. If there is trash in the parking lot, he picks it up.

Similarly, grunt-eyed managers and front liners alike at Walt Disney World and Disneyland, Chick-fil-A restaurants, Lands' End, Lexus dealerships, Enterprise Rent-A-Car, and thousands of other dedicated businesses pick up trash, polish counters, straighten displays, spruce up plants, and worry over the 101 details that together combine to make their customers' experiences with them memorable for all the right reasons.

Managers in these organizations know that it's the little service problems—small-scale neglect—that often lead to bigger ones. It's a belief that mirrors the "broken windows" theory on how to control crime first expounded by sociologists James Wilson and George Kelling in an *Atlantic Monthly* article. A broken window, graffiti-scarred building, littered sidewalk, or abandoned building does no great harm to a neighborhood if promptly fixed. But if left unaddressed, it sends a signal to criminals that no one cares about the neighborhood and encourages them to break in, vandalize, deal drugs, and more. Soon, more serious crimes like burglary, robbery, rape, and even murder begin to occur. When Rudy Giuliani was mayor of New York, he used the philosophy to great effect to clean up large parts of New York City. What is the corollary for the business world? When the details are overlooked and little things are left to fester, it can breed indifference and sloppiness on a larger level among service staff.

But attention to details involves more than just playing janitor so your people will know they should imitate your concern for what the customer sees. It also means remembering that details are at the heart of the moments of truth—those moments when the customer is in contact with your organization and forms an opinion of the quality of what you do. At Romano's Macaroni Grill, every general manager is expected to do the "little thing" of greeting and talking to customers to ensure they enjoy their visits. To Vic Pisano, the general manager of the original Macaroni Grill, simply showing you care about guests goes a long way toward creating repeat business. "You welcome everyone who comes in the door, you make sure the food is good, and you make sure the people you serve are happy," he says. The only way to do that, Pisano says, is by visiting tables and talking to customers.[19]

Manage the moments of truth well and you earn an A or a B on customers' highly subjective report cards. Ignore them, or manage them poorly, and customers give you a D or an F. Then they start looking for someone more likely to make the grade. Even more challenging is the fact that customers who grade service as a C are vulnerable to customer exit the minute someone closer, cheaper, or just plain different enters the scene.

The Service Walk

Every customer typically goes through many, many moments of truth to get a particular need met. As mentioned earlier, a moment of truth is any encounter a customer has in which he or she has an opportunity to give the organization a thumbs up or down. But it's not easy to figure out which of the hundreds of moments of truth customers experience might be *deal breakers*—interactions where the quality of service rendered has an inordinate influence on whether they decide to keep doing business with you—and which have a lesser effect on their repurchase intentions. Traditional measurement and analysis can help you zero in on customer priorities, both the large-scale kind, such as market research and detailed customer surveys, and more anecdotal and fragmented forms, like customer comment cards, surveys attached to e-mails, phone calls, and impromptu conversations with customers you meet on and off the job.

Not all moments of truth are created equal in the eyes of customers. In other words, before you make your people crazy by mandating that phones will be answered within two rings, make sure your customers consider that an important service quality factor. What impact does a quick answer have on overall satisfaction or customers' decisions to keep doing business with you? Or how about mandating that employees say "hello" to each and every customer that enters a retail business? While management might see these as vital service dimensions, customers often view it differently. View other details from the customer's standpoint as well. It will save you a lot of headaches, as well as resources spent on making improvements that have little or no effect on customer loyalty.

Defining the details in general is only a starting point. You can't manage service in absentia. You need to develop your own grunt eyes when it comes to service, making sure you walk the walk as well as talk the talk.

To take the "service walk," start by determining how your services look to your customers based on their prepurchase expectations. When you enter a bank, a car repair shop, a theater, a fast-food restaurant, a doctor's office, or an airplane, you have some notion of what ought to occur. The first thing you do is compare what's actually happening to that expectation. And when it doesn't match up, you can find yourself disoriented and confused—whether because you're dismayed or dazzled.

- If you walked into a Subway, Chick-fil-A, or McDonald's and found candles and fine china on the tables, with waiters in tuxedos hovering nearby, you'd think you were in the wrong place—or in the middle of a *Saturday Night Live* skit.

- By the same token, if you arrived for dinner at five-star Chez Ritzy and encountered the standard Burger King or McDonald's decor, menu, and service style, you would also wonder what was afoot.

From that starting point, service quality becomes a function of experience—what happens to you as the customer. That's why it's so important to see and evaluate your services the way your clients do. The math involved is relatively simple. If the experience matches their expectations, they'll judge it to be satisfactory, though hardly memorable. When it turns out differently than they expected, it becomes more memorable precisely because of its lower or higher than expected quality.

Two factors are considered by the customer: experience and outcome—what happens to them and what they get. Both must match expectations for service to be judged satisfactory; both must exceed expectations for service to be viewed as superior. But if either is substandard, the customer's combined rating will drop off the bottom of the charts.

- When the meal (outcome) is wonderful, but you have to go through hell (experience) to get it, such as waiting forever for your meal or arriving home to find items missing from a drive-thru order, the net score will be negative.
- Likewise, even when you're treated like a king by the car repair shop (experience), if your car still doesn't work properly (outcome), the net score is negative. In other words, an incompetent physical administered by a personable and humorous doctor will not satisfy. But neither will a competent physical administered by a brusque, arrogant physician—or one who hasn't bathed since the last full moon. Ditto for a cheery and courteous customer service rep who places you on hold numerous times to consult with coworkers, then eventually disconnects you, in a well-meaning but bumbling attempt to answer a question he should be able to quickly address on his own.

The caring is as important as the care to winning the customer's loyalty. You have to do both to succeed.

Dealing with Details

Many organizations put a great deal of time and energy into managing and monitoring the service outcome—the check was cashed, the operation was completed, and the account was closed. Outcomes, by and large, are easy to define and count. But paying attention to all the little details involved in the service experience is a lot tougher. It's difficult to identify and define, let alone measure and evaluate, everything the customer has to go through to get to that outcome. But that's what you, and everyone working with and for you, must learn to do as part of your service walk.

To see just how detailed your customer-level journey can be, consider the variables involved only at the points where a customer might enter your delivery processes in these various settings:

• *A Parking Lot:* Is it easy to access, well lit, clearly marked, and safe to use? Are the parking lot's users (customers) favored over the parking lot's owners (your people, especially internal VIPs)? Is it clear from wherever the customers have to park which door should be entered? Ask yourself, "If the customer's experience in the parking lot were a picture of our whole service system, what would it tell them about what we value, how we feel about customers, and where our priorities lie?"

• *An Admitting Office, a Reception Area, or a Security Check-In:* How is the area kept? Is it comfortable, clean, and user-friendly? Is it easy for customers to figure out where to go, who to see, and what to do? Are there resources, aids, supports, and guides if the customer gets confused, bored, or lost? Are such materials current and professional, or does their age qualify them as museum pieces? What is done to manage wait time? What would a picture of this scene tell the customer about the rest of the service delivery systems they'll shortly be encountering?

- *Objects, Forms, Websites, Systems, or Procedures:* Are they clearly written, professionally produced, easily navigated, and truly necessary? Will they be perceived as user friendly and customer focused or as confusing and awkwardly designed? Are there responses to negative customer reviews on the website, or are they left there to signal no one cares? Can instructions or procedures be understood by the customer without the aid of a dictionary, an interpreter, or an information technology guru? The most precious commodity for many customers today is time, and if you waste it with a confusing website design or cumbersome administrative procedures, customers probably won't return for more punishment.

- *Inbound Call Center:* Is the system large enough and sophisticated enough to handle the call load, easy to understand and use, efficient, and time effective? Must your customers negotiate their way through a long and involved voicemail system made up of seemingly endless menus of buttons to push before encountering a live human voice? Are phone encounters rushed to meet an artificial time standard, or prolonged well beyond the time the customer has allotted for your assistance due to poor staff training or a bored service rep's desire for chit chat? Is your last question to the customer a closed question (indicating a desire to stop the interaction) or an open question (communicating interest in the customer)? If the customer must be transferred, how will it feel and sound on their end of the line? Are you tracking first call resolution or first contact resolution? Remember: The first call might actually be the customer's third attempt to communicate with your company. What do they experience when they're put on hold: silence, elevator music, boring advertisements, long waits? Today, customers grade you based on the effort they must expend to deal with you.

Service Patrols

The service walk can be taken solo, but it's an equally valid tactic as something you do with one or several of your frontline people. From time to time, ask some of *them* to join you in trying on the customer's clodhoppers. Let them tell you what they see when they use their own grunt eyes to reexamine aspects of the service delivery processes and experiences that have become taken for granted over time. Ask them to point out weak spots, bottlenecks, points of both pride and embarrassment, and areas for improvement identified by customers and their own firsthand knowledge of what is involved in taking care of business.

If it's not practical to get them to accompany you, ask them to sample your service on their own. Encourage them to monitor customer review websites like Yelp. Have them critique how user friendly your website is, or ask them if they received a response to a Facebook or Twitter comment or how easy it is to access the options they need (including live help) on your voicemail system. Asking for your staff's input has the added benefit of making them feel more valued and respected.

The more you encourage frontline people to see themselves as responsible for the service experience—and the processes that make those experiences successful or difficult—the more willing and empowered they will feel to truly take care of their customers.

Jan Carlzon, architect of the well-documented service turnaround at Scandinavian Airline Systems (SAS), once summarized the journey from hip-deep red ink to basic black on the bottom line as a matter of details, details, details: "We never started out to become 1,000 percent better at anything; just 1 percent better at a thousand different things that are important to the customer—and it worked."

But at SAS, just as at USAA, Southwest Airlines, Ace Hardware, Hotel Monaco, UPS, and countless other outstanding service providers, managers continue to not only talk the talk, but walk the walk.

> You don't improve service and quality in general.
> You improve service and quality in specific.
>
> —Dr. Rodney Dueck
> Park Nicollet Medical Centers,
> Minneapolis, Minnesota

7

Learning from Lost Customers

Honest criticism is hard to take, particularly from a relative, a friend, an acquaintance, or a stranger.

—Franklin P. Jones

At first glance, putting the words "customer" and "forensics" in the same sentence might seem like a morbid oxymoron. But, lost customers can be somewhat like murdered victims— their cause of departure requires thoughtful investigation!

Forensics is the examination of evidence using a broad spectrum of disciplines to arrive at a conclusion or insight. Customer Forensics™ is typically used as a postmortem examination of hidden customer information to determine the real cause for the loss of the customer. Customer forensics also entails a timely investigation before facts and perceptions are "contaminated" by customer memory loss. The understanding gained can point the way to improvements useful in curbing future customer turnover.

A shotgun approach to customer intelligence risks completely missing the mark and often triggers lukewarm initiatives that only address symptoms. However, armed with up-to-date customer intelligence (like forensics), organizations not only can launch preventive measures to read early signals of impending customer departure, but they can also implement more efforts targeted at fixing deeper problems that contribute to customer turnover.

Police Science 101 informs us that the building blocks for solving a crime are motive, opportunity, and alibi. *Alibi* means the excuse used for not being the perpetuator was either false or not credible. *Opportunity* implies that facts put the perpetrator in a position to do the deed, and *motive* suggests that the perpetrator of the dirty deed had a reason to do it. Customer forensics uses a similar framework.

Alibi

The first step in customer forensics is to rule out all of the "natural" influencers to customer churn. Natural influences are like alibis—they can camouflage the real reason a customer leaves. The objective is to isolate those reasons that are organizationally caused. For example, if a retail store noticed an increase in sales for the month of December, conventional wisdom would suggest it was due to holiday buying. It would be important for the organization to seasonally adjust sales figures over several years to know if the real reason for a December sales increase might be something the organization did to ramp up sales.

The first "alibi analysis" technique is to look for any peaks, valleys, and patterns that may have contributed to a loss of customers. The goal is to spot aberrations in churn to discern what factors contributed to customer departures. The second data cut is to ferret out any clues that follow demographic patterns (e.g., customers primarily in a particular location, city size, climate). Similarly, ethnographic or psychographic filters can ascertain whether departed customers fit a homogenous social arrangement (e.g., more white males, more politically conservative, more single baby boomers).

Opportunity

Wise organizations look for ways to exit interview departing customers. Exit interviews create a potential opportunity to save a customer. They also create a learning opportunity at that juncture when the reasons for exiting are clear, sharp, and raw . . . not sometime much later after the customer has left when ire has dissipated and memory is hazy.

Opportunity analysis can also be enhanced with "truth syrup." Truth serum is used to get a person to disclose truth without control over what is revealed. Obviously, this would not be a positive procedure with customers! However, if you change the concept to "truth syrup," you get a more wholesome application. Customers who might otherwise be bashful about telling the real reason they departed might be incented to be more forthright. One organization held a fancy reception followed by a nonjudgmental "Be Frank" discussion with attendees, all customers who had left the organization.

Motive

Motive assessment involves direct communication with the departed customer to learn the motives for leaving. In its simplest form, it is a learning orientation rather than a sales or marketing orientation. While customer forensics insights can help shape a customer win-back strategy, their practices must never be mixed. Customer forensics takes an attitude of curiosity, discovery, and openness to divergent learning. It is a willingness to be drawn into the world of the former customer. Marketing is more about an attraction—drawing the customer to the organization.

Assessment questions focus on learning the reasons that caused customers to begin to have reservations about their relationship with your organization. They are also crafted to learn the defining incident that represented the tipping point and exit. For example, a survey question might ask: "What were the top three causes for your decision to no longer be our customer?" This question might be followed by: "Select one of the three reasons and indicate the features or actions that left you disappointed or angry?"

True motive can also come through by asking a question like: "What incident could you identify as being the final straw in your decision to leave?" Another question that can yield great insight is: "If our organization asked you to be a consultant to help us learn steps we can take to keep customers like you from leaving us, what one piece of advice would you give?"

Customer learning is a never-ending effort. Customer expectations are not only continually changing, but they are also constantly increasing. A crucial part of customer learning is the intelligence gained from those customers who leave. As the old Polish adage goes: "A guest sees more in an hour than a host sees in a year." Insider blindness can be significantly reversed by viewing the organization through the lens of former customers.

A complaining customer is my best friend.

—Stew Leonard
Stew Leonard's Dairy Stores

Imperative 3
Build a Service Vision

Yogi Berra, the immortal New York Yankee catcher, coach, and manager, is supposed to have said, "If you don't know where you're going, you're liable to end up someplace else." It's true, whether he said it or not. It is especially true of your efforts to create Knock Your Socks Off Service. Your vision of what superior service looks like is the foundation of getting where you want to go—and not "someplace else."

Building a service vision means articulating that mindset for the people who work with you. What it will take to cause customers to give you a five-star rating may be very clear in *your* mind. That is of little consequence until everyone charged with turning that vision into reality for the customer sees that vision just as clearly as you see it.

That vision—we refer to it as a "service strategy statement"—must be personally meaningful and important to everyone in the organization if it is going to become reality for the customer. That means it must not only be understandable, it must also be verifiable. Concrete standards of service quality make the vision real and palpable; regular and extensive measurement makes it meaningful.

8

The Power of a Service Strategy

Employees shouldn't be expected to deliver first-rate service if management can't first define it.

—Horst Schulze
CEO of Capella Hotels and Founder
of the Ritz-Carlton Hotel Company

A cattle rancher will tell you that moving a large herd requires bifocal vision: Without close attention to the herd, a feisty steer can double back or break away, making the rancher waste important time retrieving the malcontent. But if you don't also keep an eye on the distant gate—your ultimate destination—you may never funnel the herd through it.

When it comes to Knock Your Socks Off Service, focusing on the ultimate as well as the immediate is equally critical. "Bifocal" service vision comes from a clear focus on purpose: Defining in detail and in writing—and then repeating constantly and consistently—what your organization means when it says "Quality customer service is our goal." Your focus on purpose—your service strategy and *vision*—is your tool for aligning the day-to-day actions of your employees with the distant gate of Knock Your Socks Off Service.

All organizations have various strategies for ensuring success in the marketplace. A price strategy is laced with competitive analyses; a product strategy contains lessons learned from prototypes and test markets. A service strategy is the deliberate determination of the role that service will play in delivering value to customers. In a service-driven culture, it is typically the preeminent strategy since it contains the principles linked to growth. In other words, a great product, powerful brand, or competitive price may be the primary source of customer attraction, but the service experience is the chief reason for retention and loyalty.

Crafting a service strategy begins with the definition of the level of service an organization is committed to consistently providing to customers. Service at a Ritz-Carlton Hotel is different than service at a Hampton Inn, even though both might be great for the market or target guest served and the price point required. Once the level of service has been defined, the next step is to craft the organization's service vision. A service vision is a guide that succinctly communicates the organization's unique, distinctive service experience in the market it serves. Unlike a mission or purpose that states "who and what we are," a service vision focuses on the customer side of the business with a goal of communicating a clear vision of "what we strive to be famous for in the eyes of our customers." It is a tool for driving customer value into the heart of the organization.

Being excellent at customer service is not about what organizations claim; it is about how their customers consistently experience the organization. When consulting firm Bain and Company asked the senior leaders of a large number of major companies if they believed their company delivered a superior proposition to their customers, 80 percent indicated that they did. However, only 8 percent of their customers agreed with them.[20]

Choosing a Service Strategy

Let's pretend you want to open a competitive shoe store. You pick the perfect location and a clever name for your company. But, one of the first key decisions you must make is the breadth and diversity of your product offering. Are you going to carry both sports and dress shoes? High-end or budget-pleasing shoes, or both? Shoes for a certain market but not others? Shoes produced by one, several, or many shoe makers? Will you specialize in hard-to-find shoes or hard-to-fit customers? All of these product strategy decisions will impact your success with the market you hope to serve.

Service is less about product and more about experience. Instead of being an "object seller," you become a "memory maker." And, the choice of the strategy you select will impact just how big a positive memory you create. Consider this: You might not remember your last trip to the grocery store, post office, or retail website, but with the right intensity of focus zeroed in on the experience you create, you can turn a ho-hum, same-old-same-old incident into a delightful, memory-making encounter.

Just as customer loyalty is a much higher level of affinity than simply customer satisfaction (think Nordstrom versus Sears) and customer devotion is even a higher level above customer loyalty (think Lexus versus Jaguar), we consider customer centric to be the pinnacle of dedication to the customer by an organization. It reflects the intensity and pervasiveness of an organization's focus on the customer. The less the customer's experience dominates how an organization is led and managed, the lower the customer's evaluation. One way to think about the intensity and pervasiveness of focus is by using the labels that follow. The organization that lives, eats, and sleeps a great customer experience is likely to have a very different positive memory-making success than an organization that views the customer more as a necessary interruption to their preferred focus.

Customer Centric	Customer Focused	Customer Friendly	Customer Aware	Customer Indifferent

Let's examine each of the five customer strategies in more detail. Keep in mind that having a poor customer reputation is likely to be the result of a series of decisions even if it is a decision to be negligent or inattentive.

Customer indifference is a dangerous characterization by customers. Indifference is not viewed as uncaring; it is seen as arrogant—one of the traits most loathed by customers. Organizations that are hostile to customers do not remain in business. There might be a few examples of highly inwardly focused organizations that can be antagonistic toward customers and hang on for a long time. Some public institutions might be painted with such a "customer hostile" brush. Most do not regularly mistreat customers as much as they remain uninterested in the customer's needs or issues. Customers avoid such organizations if at all possible and repeatedly speak ill of them to others.

Customer aware cultures are those that are aware of the customer since they are reminded of their presence via frequent complaints. However, their overall attitude is one of accommodation rather than support. This can be found in highly regulated industries that are preoccupied with the regulation to the exclusion of the customer's experience. Think of many discount retail stores, fast-food restaurants, and some modes of public transportation. Policies and practices are crafted for organizational convenience even if they leave customers confused and/or frustrated. These organizations typically survive if they lack competition or if they have a product, price, or convenience that customers desire and simply put up with the poor service in order to get it. Their customers are often consistently disappointed with their experience.

Customer friendly is a label reserved for organizations that give enough lip service to customer service that it shows up in pockets of service delivery, but not consistently. A typical bank might be one example, with a friendly branch in one location and another branch simply going through the motions. It might be found in a moderately priced retail store where sales clerks are polite and respectful, but far from assertive. They often complain to customers about their own company's rules or procedures. The stance yields customers who are generally satisfied. Satisfied customers only remain as long as a better option is unavailable; they essentially take the organization for granted! Customer-friendly organizations can survive if they can keep the price-service-product (or outcome) in proper balance. However, such organizations are vulnerable to the appearance of a competitor offering a better product or outcome, cheaper price, or better service.

Customer-focused cultures are found in organizations that get consistently good marks from their customers. They not only do the basics exceedingly well, but they also periodically take actions that yield a great story customers enjoy repeating. They place extensive effort on ensuring that offerings are based on up-to-date customer intelligence and feedback. They ensure employees are resourced, supported, empowered, and motivated. They ensure service is comfortable and convenient. Leaders spend time in the field; customer experience metrics are valued; and customer-facing units are well trained in customer-handling manners. Their efforts produce customers who are dependably loyal.

Customer-centric cultures are rare. A positive customer experience is almost guaranteed. Leaders' obsession with superior service dominates their agendas, priorities, and accolades. Employees seem to have unlimited authority to take care of customers and exercise obvious initiative to ensure customers get a consistently great experience. Enormous effort is placed on training and continuous improvement. These organizations hire the best, expect the best performance, treat their employees as the best, and hold leaders accountable for achieving the best. Their over-the-top service creates a strong, almost cult-like following among customers. Their customers enthusiastically speak of them in terms that reflect devotion, even love.

Obviously, customers enjoy the service performance that typically comes from a customer-centric organization. However, as any responsible chief financial officer (CFO) can tell you, there are more components to success than the customer's evaluation on the quality of the service they receive. L.L. Bean and Starbucks depend on a good product to go with the customer's experience. Lexus and Trader Joe's count on having showrooms and grocery stores in the right location to reach their target customer. USAA Insurance and Amazon.com depend on great information systems to support their super-friendly customer contact people. Great customer service can only go so far in covering mediocrity in other aspects of the value proposition.

There is also the issue of the economics of operation. If a budget hotel decided to start delivering customer-centric service like that found in a luxury hotel, it not only might irresponsibly exceed their customers' requirements, it might also bankrupt the hotel. We expect to get great service when we pay extremely high prices. This is not to say that great service is reliant on high prices, as both Zappos.com and Lands' End have proven. It is simply that if a high price is paid by the customer, the customer's expectations elevate with the investment he or she makes. There is also the issue of the role that great customer service plays in gaining competitive advantage. When Lexus tries to one up Infiniti, it is more likely customer service that tips the scale for consumers. Wise organizations must examine an array of components that make up their unique offering juxtapositioned against other operating factors (opportunities, threats, costs, etc.) and then decide the proper level of service to pursue.

Crafting a Service Vision

Your organization probably has a mission statement. That's great. But to keep your unit focus sharp, you need your own well-defined, carefully worded service *vision* statement. Your statement may be unique to your unit or a variation on the organization's central strategy. It should contain a profile of your core customer base, describe what you do that is of value to them, and explain how you—and they—will know it when your goal of customer delight is achieved. It should also clarify the aspects of your service approach that separate you from competitors in customers' eyes.

Customers relish consistency. Texas A&M researcher Leonard Berry and colleagues found that the number one attribute customers value in the service they receive is *reliability*—your ability to provide what was promised, dependably and accurately. Customers want the service from branch A to be as good as branch B; they don't like having to choose a specific location—or a specific teller, floor salesperson, or waiter—because opting for others represents a roll of the dice. We want them all to be effective. How do you get everyone in the organization "rowing together as one" to deliver a consistently high level of service? It starts with a compelling and actionable service vision.

Defining what you are trying to ultimately accomplish with and for customers helps your people understand the rhyme and reason of the work they do. Your service vision statement should be so well defined that your people always know which side to come down on when they face decisions about how to provide truly superior service. It's not magic. It's simply the power of purpose.

Your service vision statement, when done well, will:

- Ensure that everyone in your unit is working with the same idea of "what's important around here."
- Act as the "lens" through which front liners view every decision they make or action they take that impacts customers.
- Help individual employees understand the rationale behind organizational policy so they have confidence in resolving unique and unusual situations.
- Serve as the foundation for service standards, norms, metrics, and aligned processes.
- Describe what makes your approach to service distinct in the marketplace.
- Provide a tool for aligning strategy and effort so customers enjoy consistency and reliability in service quality.

Here's what our research has found about the "power of purpose" in creating Knock Your Socks Off Service:

- If you do not have a definition of what good service means, your chances of getting high marks from your customers are about three in ten.
- If you have a very general definition, your chances of getting high marks from your customers improve to about 50/50.

- If you have a detailed definition of what good service means—if it is defined in the context of both the *company* and the *customer*, if it is well communicated to employees, and if it is tied to specific standards and measures—your chances of getting high marks from your customers are close to 90 percent.

Helping Employees Focus

A service vision statement isn't something simply to hang on the wall or pass out on laminated wallet cards. Once it exists, there are a multitude of ways to give it life and power.

- *Test decisions against your service vision.* Enlist one, two, perhaps even all of your employees to give you feedback on the consistency between your actions and the vision statement. And thank them for their help!
- *Ask front liners to use it to evaluate your unit's policies, procedures, and general "ways of doing things."* Are they consistent with the vision? Do they really help get things done for the customers? If not, where do they interfere with giving good service? And how can they be changed?
- *Hold "what's stupid around here?" meetings.* Use the vision statement to help identify outmoded practices, time-wasters, repeated trouble spots, and customer-vexing aspects of your business that make you look dumb to your customers—and each other.
- *Set "stop, start, and measure" objectives.* Perhaps once a quarter, ask every employee to come with a list of items under three headings:
  1. Things we should stop doing around here
  2. Things we should start doing around here
  3. Things we don't track or measure—but should
- *Hold a "focus fantasy" meeting with your employees.* Ask your people to discuss who they would like to be like: If they could model the business in general and their behaviors in particular after a famous or respected organization, who

would it be and why? Universal Orlando? Virgin Airlines? The Container Store? In-N-Out Burger? Cadillac? Their neighborhood grocer or hardware store? Or discuss what you would have to do differently to make the cover of the leading trade journal in your industry. Then act on what you hear.

The power of purpose is the power of knowing what to do, and when and how to do it, without having to be told. It helps your people take control of their work and frees them from the adolescent dependence on "management" that characterizes too many businesses today. It allows you to stop acting like a parent and start working with your people as adults.

If you use your service vision as a lens through which to look from the inside out, you should see the things that customers value and can set your organization apart. If you use it as a lens to look from the outside in, you should get a consistent service focus that helps your people to work in "sync," with their actions in alignment with strategic goals.

> If you don't know where you are going, any road will take you there.
>
> —David Campbell
> Industrial Psychologist

9

Getting Your Vision Down on Paper

Good business leaders create a vision, articulate the vision, passionately own the vision, and relentlessly drive it to completion.

—Jack Welch
retired CEO of GE

A good service vision statement involves customers *and* employees. It takes on tangible shape and form when you actually put it on paper where everyone can see and use it. As you work to define your vision, it's important not to overlook two key resources:

- Customers are not only highly qualified, but generally willing to provide input that will help a company figure out what it wants and doesn't want, how it does and doesn't want it delivered, and what elements of the service experience could be changed, improved, or removed for the business to serve them better.
- Frontline employees are armed with an incredible amount of untapped information about customers and the types of service that leave a lasting, *positive* impression on them. And they know from firsthand experience where the weak spots and fail points are in even the most meticulously designed service delivery processes.

Words with Meaning

A service vision statement should be able to pass four quick tests:

1. It should be clear, concise, and understandable. Dilbert defines a vision statement as a "long awkward sentence that demonstrates management's inability to think clearly." Make sure you prove the notorious cartoon character wrong.
2. It should communicate, in actionable ways, the things you need to do to satisfy, impress, and keep your customers.
3. It should be consistent with other things you tell employees about the organization's mission, brand promise, and purpose.
4. It should pass the employee "snicker test": Reading it, whether on paper or out loud, should help your people better understand what to do, how to do it, and why to do it, not make them giggle, guffaw, and roll their eyes heavenward. It's important that the service vision be ambitious yet grounded in reality, and not written as if it's an advertising slogan.

Remember: Knock Your Socks Off Service is mostly a person-to-person activity. If your statement of service focus doesn't make it crystal clear how you want customers to feel (happy, entertained, secure, cared about, or like they're dealing with professionals), it isn't complete.

No Put-On at the Ritz

When you see a service vision statement done well, you just know it makes sense and helps in everything from measurement to motivation. Consider, for example, Ritz-Carlton Hotels, a two-time winner of the Malcolm Baldrige National Quality Award. The company's service vision was put into words before the first property opened in 1983, almost thirty years ago. Horst Schulze, then president and chief operating officer (COO), and his senior managers believed that employees couldn't be expected to deliver first-rate, five-star service if management couldn't define it.

A good part of what Schulze and his management team came up with is embodied in the sixty-three-word statement of the Ritz-Carlton Credo and the twenty "Ritz-Carlton Basics" that define Knock Your Socks Off Service at the Ritz (Figure 9-1).

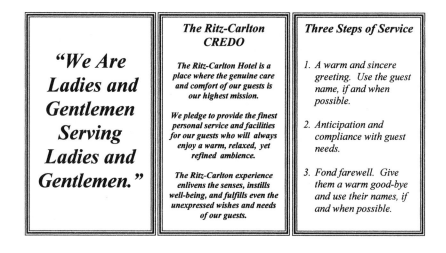

Figure 9-1. Ritz Carlton Credo.

The service vision is captured by their credo: *"We pledge to provide the finest personal service and facilities for our guests who will always enjoy a warm, relaxed yet refined ambiance. The Ritz-Carlton experience enlivens the senses, instills well-being and fulfills even the unexpressed wishes and needs of our guests."*

The hotel also found it useful to craft a sound bite as a pneumonic—"We are ladies and gentlemen serving ladies and gentlemen"—to help employees remember the experience they consistently want to create for guests.

Notice how the Ritz-Carlton service standards—the twenty Basics—are aligned with the credo. For example, the vision describes creating a "warm, relaxed yet refined ambiance," which is made actionable for employees with the service standard, "use proper vocabulary with our guests." At the Ritz-Carlton, casual language like "okay" and "no problem" is replaced with a more refined vernacular like "my pleasure" or "certainly" to match the environment. The idea isn't to come off as stuffy or aristocratic, but rather to match the luxurious and professional setting. As Horst Schulze was fond of saying, "Elegance without warmth is arrogance."

Transforming Words to Action

Three steps are integral to formulating the service vision:

• *Identify your key customers.* For Courtyard by Marriott Hotels, it's the business traveler, a group that accounts for most of the hotel's business. That doesn't mean Courtyard won't jump to serve other customer groups. It just means the hotel's service vision—"we make it our business to know business travelers"—and delivery processes are designed and managed in a way that ensures that the key customer group receives the customized care and amenities (e.g., high-speed Internet access, ample work space in rooms, big continental breakfast to start the day) to keep it happy and returning again and again.

• *Identify your core contribution to customers.* For airlines, it's moving things from point A to point B, on time, safely, with luggage intact and ideally on the same plane as the passenger who brought it to the airport. For a printing company, it's meeting the customer's need for high-quality documents that are produced on time and within budgets. In essence, your core contributions are the things you absolutely have to perform well to stay in the business you're in.

• *Decide what you want to be famous for.* A service vision ought to have some "jump start" component that makes you distinctive and exciting in the eyes of customers. Nordstrom is well-known for its return policy, Zappos.com for how they personalize the buying experience for repeat customers, and outdoor gear store REI for its interactive, "try before you buy" sales approach and customer education. Typically, this is where there can be a clear and distinguishable difference between you and your competition.

Once you've formulated your service vision, you must communicate it over and over again. Just as 20/20 vision doesn't help the person who won't watch where he or she is going, your service vision will mean nothing unless you and your employees can articulate, translate, and act on it.

A Service Vision Statement Sampler

To help you craft your own service vision statement, we offer several examples. Notice that they come in all lengths, styles, shapes, and sizes. Yours may resemble several, one, or none of them. What matters is that your statement fits your business strategy, culture, and customers.

If brevity is the soul of wit, it's worth measuring the words you use carefully and making them count, not mount up. Here's how some companies, including a convention and exposition management company, an auto auction wholesaler, a restaurant, a large hospital, a university, a senior living company, and a consulting firm, "cut to the chase."

Freeman
"To support exhibitors, show managers and event professionals in the successful marketing of their products

and services by providing highly personalized, proactive solutions delivered through a valued relationship with trusted, accessible experts."

Do it right. First time. Every time.

Manheim
"We are a team of success-makers—for customers, partners and each other. Our integrity and passion fuel us; our values and legacy guide us, and our commitment to proactive and personalized service unites us."

Fueled by employees; driven for customers.

Quaker Steak and Lube
"Our guests will have fun, feel the energy, experience unique tastes and know we care."

It's more fun to eat in a saloon than to drink in a restaurant.

Aurora St. Luke's
"We are committed to setting the standards of excellence in our profession and our markets. Our innovative technology and progressive attitude attract patients, staff and physicians. Our personalized care and service ensure they return and recommend us to others."

National Hispanic University
"We are driven by the transformational power of education. Focused on student success through a professional and personalized approach, our passionate and culturally rich familia inspires those we serve to lead."

¡Creando Líderes! (We create leaders!)

Arbor Company
"As a community of care givers we are here for one purpose: to engage and enrich the health and spirit of our residents. We honor individuality and celebrate each person's unique life through deep connections with our residents and families. We create delightful surprises

and meaningful moments within a safe and caring community."

We listen, we respond, we care.

Banco de Finanzas (Nicaragua)
"We are a dynamic, entrepreneurial team and passionately committed towards building long-lasting relationships with our clients, by making the way easy so they can reach their dreams. We put every effort in exceeding the expectation of those who we service, by valuing their time and making sure their experience with BDF is reliable, transparent and pleasurable."

Chip Bell Group
"The service vision of The CHIP BELL Group is to provide selected clients with relevant service wisdom they experience as incredibly empowering and surprisingly simple that is delivered through a valued partnership."

Sometimes articulating the whats, whys, and wherefores of your service strategy seems almost painfully simple—only after, of course, you've completed the often arduous process of crafting it.

As short and simple as many of the best service vision statements are, many companies abbreviate them even further as a means of helping embed them in employees' minds. Walk through Dell Computer's headquarters in Round Rock, Texas, for example, and it's hard to miss one phrase adorning conference rooms and hallways: "The Customer Experience: Own It."[21] Consider creating your own service vision "sound bite" to help guide and inform employees' everyday actions with customers.

Where there is no vision, the people perish.

—Ecclesiastes

10

Service Standards Build Consistency

In essence, if we want to direct our lives, we must take control of our consistent actions. It's not what we do once in a while that shapes our lives, but what we do consistently.

—Anthony Robbins

While a *service vision* describes the experience you want to *create* for customers, *a service standard* communicates *expectations* of the attitudes, beliefs, and values—what we strive to *be*—in sync with the service vision to be delivered every time in a similar fashion across the organization. A *service norm* describes the actions, practices, and behaviors—what we strive to *do*—that ensure customers get consistent action, effort, or execution. It is the *evidence*.

For example, if the service *standard* is "we provide our customers access that is easy and quick, and ensure rapid response to questions or problems" (what employees strive to be), a service *norm* might read, "all associates will be reachable by phone during business hours unless in flight or directly engaged with a customer; all phone calls from customers are returned within the hour, and all e-mails answered within four hours of receipt" (what employees strive to do).

Why bother creating service standards and norms? For one, they help translate a service vision into concrete goals that your people can easily understand and work toward every day. Standards and norms are also important tools for aligning the organization so that everyone is "rowing together as one." When specific, measurable, and perceived as ambitious but achievable by service staff, standards become a powerful means of communicating performance expectations.

Service standards also help create a consistent experience that builds all-important customer trust. Whether promising package delivery "absolutely, positively" overnight, guaranteeing credit decisions on home mortgage applications within a week, or guaranteeing responses to customer phone calls within two hours, regularly living up to the "service promise" builds credibility and creates a bond with customers that becomes a foothold to customer loyalty.

When people know what to expect each and every time they do business with you—caring, knowledgeable, and competent employees that won't let them walk away unhappy—they are more likely to return again with their funds and friends in tow. But if you're seen as erratic and unpredictable—some days delivering on the service promise, and other days treating standards as "nice to" but not "need to" performance goals—it creates a sense of unease and distrust that has a corrosive effect on loyalty.

Build Standards around Loyalty Factors

The best service standards strike the right balance between customer expectations and internal capabilities. Set the bar too low and you risk offending customers; set it too high and it can frustrate and demoralize employees who, despite their best efforts, regularly fall short of the mark.

When it comes to responsiveness standards, for example, it's a mistake to think customers won't accept anything less than "right this instant." On the other hand, giving yourself too much extra wiggle room can make you look slow and indifferent in relation to more nimble competitors.

Start the standards-building process by surveying customers to find out what separates *exemplary* from *satisfactory* performance in their minds, whether it be how quickly you re-solve their problems; order delivery expectations; response time to phone calls, e-mails, or tweets; or time on hold.

In the dry-cleaning business, for example, there's a big difference between "I have to have this dry cleaning to wear next week," and "I want to have these winter clothes cleaned before I put them away for the season." Use that information to create standards that work well for you and then try them out on customers. Then get their feedback via formal and in-formal surveys to find out if that timeliness standard works for them. If it doesn't, you can work together to find an alternative.

You'll also want to determine performance thresholds—service areas where, if performance consistently falls below a certain expectation, customers would strongly consider taking their business elsewhere. When sending an e-mail on a company's information site, most customers would prefer to hear back within an hour or two, but depending on the urgency of the request, they might be fine with a satisfactory response on that same day. But if you wait until the next day or two to reply, and do so more than once, then it becomes a significant black mark against your organization, pushing customers ever closer to aligning with a more responsive competitor.

Work first to create standards in areas that your customer research shows have the biggest influence on customer loyalty. Clients may not care that you guarantee to answer the phone in two rings instead of three—they'd much rather you ensure that whoever picks up on that third ring is equipped to handle their question or solve their problem on first contact, in a friendly and efficient manner.

A Moving Target

Setting service standards and norms isn't a one-time proposi-tion. Customer expectations are constantly in motion, and the more exposure your clients have to service role models, the more rapidly their expectations change. Regular clients of

FedEx, accustomed to its exemplary delivery performance and ability to track packages by the minute, will expect more of the same when they order from your website or catalog. Customers of Travelocity or USAA Insurance, who are used to having their questions answered and problems resolved on first contact (and not pulling out their hair trying to find a human being to talk to), won't look kindly on calling your organization and getting passed from Patti to Paul to Penelope—or trapped in voicemail hell—before finally getting someone who can help them. Those who frequent Amazon.com or Zappos.com will expect to receive immediate e-mail confirmation of orders they've placed on your e-commerce site, as well as acknowledgment of any other e-contact ("we have received your e-mail. . .") within moments of sending it—and sometimes detailed responses to their questions within that same time frame.

These escalated expectations may not mean you have to equal the performance of service exemplars, but it does mean you'll have to elevate your performance to stay competitive and keep these newly enlightened customers coming back for more.

The bottom line is to make sure your standards for response time to customers via social media or e-mail are pegged to "Internet time," not the rhythms of your own internal company systems. It's a message organizations would do well to remember when creating standards for any facet of their customer service performance.

Standards and Norms in Action

Banco Popular North America, a Chicago, Illinois-based bank, has developed a reputation for impressive service quality and progressive people practices that have led to honors like being named one of *Fortune* magazine's "100 Best Companies to Work For" in 2005.

We've included a selection of the bank's service standards and norms, along with its service vision, to illustrate how those three elements—when well-constructed and aligned—lay the foundation for creating Knock Your Socks Off Service. Banco Popular, like other customer-centric organizations, understands that unless standards and norms are clearly written, specific, and measurable—and employees are consistently held accountable for achieving them—they are little more than empty promises or slogans hanging on the wall.

Banco Popular's Service Vision

"We are here for one purpose: to deliver consistently engaging and caring experiences for our customers. Their needs and dreams drive us, their challenges unite us, and our values guide us in delivering trusted financial solutions. Our dream makers' [what the bank calls its employees] pride and passion are contagious."

Standards and Norms

People Standard: Dream makers are dedicated, resourceful, and caring people who share and demonstrate our values and commitment for the customer and each other.
  Norms: Our people:

- Are team oriented and believe in our mission and embrace our diversity and heritage.
- Look for ways to add value to the customer *and* the bank.
- Use sound judgment in making decisions on behalf of the customer *and* the bank.

Communications Standard: Our communication is timely, clear, and consistent.
  Norms: We:

- Never use e-mail or voicemail when we need to have a personal conversation.
- Communicate clearly about deliverables to manage expectations.
- Help our people "connect the dots" by including the "why" in communications.

Responsiveness Standard: We respond with a sense of urgency to our customers and coworkers.
   Norms: We:

- Respond to customer calls within one hour; internal phone calls or e-mails within the same day.
- Provide solutions or updates the next business day.
- When out of the workplace on business, we check daily for customer calls or e-mails and respond or delegate accordingly on the same day.

Accuracy Standard: We do it right the first time, every time.
   Norms: We:

- Treat every transaction as if it were our own or that of a beloved family member.
- Clarify and confirm requests to ensure we understand the need and we execute with precision.
- Are thorough and complete in everything we do.

Accountability Standard: Each of us is accountable to ensure every interaction with a customer or coworker is managed in a positive and purposeful way.
   Norms: We:

- Treat every customer as if Roberto (the bank's president) sent them to us.
- Own and stay connected to the customer's request from beginning to end and then follow-up, being accountable for the outcome. We are "links in a chain" working together for the benefit of the customer.
- Act in the best interest of the customer and build trust by personally facilitating any necessary hand-off (to a coworker).

Consistency Breeds Trust

Service standards and norms are a pledge to customers that you'll be the same reliable and responsive organization each time they do business with you, and not blow hot or cold depending on management's fickle agenda—"last month we focused on service, this month we're back to productivity"— or the state of the last quarterly financial report. Tying standards to performance factors that have the biggest impact on customer loyalty, then being vigilant in measuring, adjusting, and delivering on them to ensure you meet customers' shifting expectations, is one of the surest ways to build customer trust—and to create distinction in your industry.

Consistency is the foundation of virtue.

—Francis Bacon

Imperative 4

Make Your Service Delivery Processes ETDBW (Easy to Do Business With)

Your service delivery process is the apparatus, physical and procedural, that the employees of your organization must have at their disposal to meet customers' needs and to keep the service promises you make to your customers. A well-designed service delivery process will make you easy to do business with. What your service strategy promises is what your process must deliver. Every time.

If your promise is "twenty-four-hour delivery on all orders—no exceptions," your service delivery process is everything you do and use to make twenty-four-hour delivery a reality, from your order entry system to the way you measure your performance.

In a badly designed and poorly operating delivery process, you frequently hear *managers* complaining about lazy, unmotivated employees; *frontline employees* complaining about stupid, unreasonable customers; and *customers* complaining about inflexible, unhelpful people and rules. A well-done service delivery process is customer and employee friendly and has monitors and feedback mechanisms to enable the people who work in the process to correct poor results.

Your continuing quest should be to seek out ways of making it easier for your customers to do business with you tomorrow than it was for them to do business with you last year, last month, last week, and last night.

Rest assured, that's exactly what your competition is doing.

11

Effort: The Achilles' Heel of Customer Experience

The less effort, the faster and more powerful you will be.

—Bruce Lee, actor

A consultant with an inoperative computer is much like a taxi driver with his cab in the shop. Chip's sick computer needed a particular part to get him back in business. Now, get ready to follow his experience with the hellish computer part replacement process.

A call to the computer manufacturer's toll-free number led to an automated phone queue followed by a wait, followed by a "too-many-questions" service clerk, followed by a transfer and wait, followed by a tech support person, followed by a transfer and wait, followed by the correct tech support person, followed by a long wait, followed by the part arriving ground instead of overnight, followed by the part arriving broken.

So, how are you feeling? The super long sentence in the previous paragraph was crafted to demonstrate the customer's side of the encounter. We have all been there. And, it reminds us that customer effort trumps just about every other service factor these days.

Convergys, a research company based in Cincinnati, Ohio, found that customers who rated their experience as satisfactory *and* easy were three times more loyal than those who simply stated they were "completely satisfied" with the experience. The *Harvard Business Review* reports in a study of more than 75,000 B2B and B2C customers that "When it comes to service, companies create loyal customers primarily by helping them solve their problems quickly and easily."

We were conducting a series of focus groups for a large client to ascertain what service factors were deemed most important by their customers. One technique used was paired comparison. You can put twenty factors on a sheet of paper and ask respondents to rank order them. However, you get a far more accurate picture of priority if respondents are asked to look at each factor paired with every other factor to select which is more important. Applying a simple regression analysis to the data led to a true picture of customer preference. "Easy to do business with" was more important than smart people, empowered people, friendly people, accuracy, reliability, great service recovery, knows me and my needs, etc.

Focus groups enable a researcher to get underneath data to ferret out the meaning behind the responses—something a survey cannot accomplish. We wanted to learn what "easy to do business with" was really about in the eyes of these customers. We were confident that learning the "whys" behind the "whats" could surface a solution that dealt with the cause and not the symptom. What we learned was straight out of your Anthropology 101 textbook. Customers examined "service" effort through the lens of time, values, language, traditions, and symbols.

Customer Anthropology and Effort

Social or cultural anthropologists study the dynamics of groups with a particular frame of reference. Just like a physician has a model of a "healthy body" in mind as he or she examines for gaps between what is and what should be, anthropologists attempt to understand a culture by considering their allegiances to time, values, language, traditions, and symbols. The mosaic provides a path to an enriched understanding (Figure 11-1).

Figure 11-1. Components of Effort.

Time

Anyone who has traveled to the Caribbean learns quickly about being "on island time." A feature of the island culture is to slow down. Customers also view effort in terms of time. When the customer feels the pace is slower than their service clock suggests it should be, it starts their satisfaction meter in the wrong direction. It means knowing the customer's service clock and matching it.

Or, it means reframing their expectation of wait by altering their perception of time. Disney tells you the wait time in the queue for park rides—all set to be less actual time than posted time. They also entertain us as a means to alter our perception of wait. A branch bank polls its lobby customers on what they prefer to watch on the television monitor viewable from the teller line should the line get longer than expected. Find out what time means to your customers and manage that part of effort that is exacerbated by disappointments around time.

Values

Cultures have always been defined in part by what is valued by their people. Customers are no different. And, while all customers are different, they share certain core values. Queues in airports, restaurants, and the Department of Motor Vehicles are generally orderly without pushing and shoving because of a shared value of fairness—as in, "no cutting in line" and "first come, first served." We expect folks in first class to get better food than airline passengers in coach. And, as passengers, we also know that first class seats are the result of frequent-flyer loyalty or the price of the ticket and not due to any socioeconomic, gender, or racial factors.

Effort is also a critical component of value. The recession has elevated customers' standards for the level of effort they will tolerate before becoming unhappy. Pay attention to dissonant messaging. When customers hear, "Your call is very important to us" followed by another message that says, "Your wait time is approximately thirty minutes," they do not interpret it as rude; they see it as a bold-faced lie. A business that closes earlier than what is posted on the front door or a computer part promised overnight that is shipped ground crosses the value line for customers and spells deception, not bad manners. Make certain you know the true meaning of values related to service among your customers. Just guessing or assuming "they are just like me" will lead you astray.

Language

Language is not just about communication—with its idioms and slang. It is about how meaning is transmitted from brain to brain. And, the mental pictures created by the words chosen are fraught with the potential for inaccuracy and misinterpretation. The conduit that drives the picture exchange hangs on effective and caring listening. So, how good are service providers at really listening? According to Convergys research, 45 percent of customers think companies do not have a good understanding of what their customers really experience when dealing with them. Yet, 80 percent of employees and executives think they understand.[22] How could that be?

When resource-strapped employees are placed in a listening role—whether face to face or ear to ear—the risk of misinterpretation and error soars. It results in employees focusing on the task, not the solution, and robotic adherence to policies and procedures rather than effective problem solving. It also results in undue effort by customers who are forced to emote, evade, echo, or escalate just to get what they want. Make great listening a vital part of the organization's DNA. And, remember the ancient line, "You are not eligible to change someone's view until you demonstrate you understand his or her view!"

Traditions

Traditions are the customs, mores, and habits shared by a society. For instance, Western culture is keenly concerned with human rights and equal opportunity, whereas other cultures are not. Customers also share a set of mores. As customers, we expect service to be a form of assistance. We assume we will be treated with respect. We anticipate a service provider will be there when we need them and in the form that we require. Excess effort surfaces when the practice of service fails to jive with the expectancy of service.

Today, customers expect access around the clock, not just from nine to five, Monday through Friday. While they enjoy the access and time-saving aspect of self-service and automation, when it fails to work, customers feel abandoned and devalued unless given an easy, quick back door to a person. They assume service will be crafted to fit their needs and they will not be shoehorned into a service delivery process without flexibility. They expect a wide array of choices and abhor any offering that is solely "one size fits all." This means that the perfect customer experience requires knowing what customers expect and ensuring the traditions of service match their requirements.

Symbols

Few things characterize a culture more than the symbols it employs. Most Americans above the age of five can correctly identify Abe Lincoln, the American eagle or flag, the Statue of Liberty, or Uncle Sam. Symbols make us feel secure and reduce the anxiety of uncertain situations and encounters. They are the emotional sign posts that help us feel a sense of belonging. Customers use symbols for many of the same reasons.

Effort surfaces when the signals of service send a different message than customers anticipate. When John Longstreet (now CEO of Quaker Steak and Lube) was general manager of a large hotel, he set up periodic focus groups with the taxi drivers that transported his guests to the airport after their stay. He learned about subtle symbols derived from the guests' sights, sounds, and smells rarely found on a guest comment card. Missing toilet items signaled poor accuracy; scorched-smelling towels implied the potential for a hotel fire; and a poorly lighted parking lot brought worries about safety in hotel hallways.

When famed anthropologist Margaret Mead first visited Samoa in the South Pacific, it led her to write in the preface of her book *Coming of Age in Samoa*, "Courtesy, modesty, good manners, conformity to definite ethical standards are universal. . . . It is instructive to know that standards differ in the most unexpected ways." Her nonjudgmental approach to the target of her research enabled her to gain a level of intimacy with Samoan inhabitants that few researchers had been able to attain.

There are many components in the social encounter we call service. As service providers, how can we be effective at learning precisely how time, values, language, traditions, and symbols are embedded in our customers' experiences? We can take the Mead approach—nonjudgmental recognition that customer "standards differ in the most unexpected ways." How are you gaining customer insight into your customers' anthropology? How can you utilize that customer intelligence to remove and manage service effort?

> Anthropology demands the open-mindedness with which one must look and listen, record in astonishment and wonder that which one would not have been able to guess.
>
> —Margaret Mead

12

Making Service Delivery Processes "Happy"

You can take great people, highly trained and motivated, and put them in a lousy system and the system
will win every time.

—Geary Rummler
Founding Partner,
Performance Design Lab

The Native Americans believed every creation had a soul.
A tree possessed a spirit in the same way as a horse, bird, or
human being, which engendered a feeling of oneness with
nature and a focus on conservation. While the buffalo was
killed for its meat and other uses, it was also revered for
having a great spirit.

Organizations that create consistently loyal customers look
at their service processes in a similar way. While they know, of
course, that an order entry process is not "alive," thinking of it
in that fashion—as a living, feeling, organic system—helps ensure it is designed and maintained in a way that best serves the
organizational "tribe" of customers and employees.

A "live" perspective ensures key service processes receive
the proper care and feeding so they don't fall into disrepair and

consistently deliver the kind of hassle-free, friendly service experiences that create distinction in the market.

Service Processes Defined

Service processes can be defined from two perspectives. From the inside of the organization looking out, they are a collection of procedures and practices that constitute and govern a complete service encounter. From the outside looking in—the customer's perspective—processes are the steps (and sometimes hoops) companies "put customers through" to get the products or services they need.

A hotel has a process for check-in. From the customer's perspective, this more often than not begins when he or she approaches the front desk to check in and ends when he or she checks out and leaves the hotel. However, for the hotel, the process might begin with reservations or someone alerting the front desk that the hotel was overbooked. And it might not end until the night audit has done an operational review and balanced the shift. There are many process steps invisible to customers that need to be well designed and executed to ensure good end-to-end service experiences.

Cumbersome service processes are the bane of customer loyalty. Let's face it, most customers would prefer to simply snap their fingers and instantly get the product or outcome they desire. Of course, we can imagine some masochistic customers who simply can't get enough bureaucracy, irritating paperwork, or exasperating delays ("I only stopped by to see if you had some more forms I could fill out" or "I called for one reason—so you could put me on hold again!").

A process might be governed by a set a procedures (fill out the application in triplicate or listen to ten voice response unit options before making a choice), a collection of regulations (complete in one hour and provide a copy to security), or even certain laws (enter into the company ledger). But although the primary role of processes is to ensure service is delivered in a consistent and efficient fashion, there is no bylaw stating they should also make customers want to pull their hair out.

How to Make a Service Delivery Process "Happy"

What do we mean by a *"happy"* process?

The term *happy process* originated with one of our international clients. We were grappling with a way to explain the meaning of process alignment as a part of developing company-wide service standards and norms. Our client thought about the end result and suggested that one outcome of alignment might be "happy processes"—procedures and practices designed in a way that created a kind of unexpected joy for customers and employees because of their simplicity or ease of use as viewed through the customers' eyes. Think also of what would make a process happy if it could come alive—it would work well, it would work well with other processes, it would make a difference, and it would gain the admiration of its caretaker. The label proved to be a powerful metaphor that greatly contributed to helping employees understand the desired outcome of a company-wide process alignment effort.

There are a number of principles for creating happy processes. Remember, a happy process works hard for everyone—the customer, employees, leaders, the organization, as well as "fellow" processes. What follows are seven principles for happy service process management.

1. *Processes must be viewed from the customers' perspective.* The customers' perspective trumps processes built for internal convenience every time. A financial services client of ours was going through the first steps in developing service standards when the CEO heard about the excessive wait times customers were experiencing due to limited levels of authority mandated for branch employees. No one was certain when and/or why these levels of authority existed other than they had been around a long time. When questioned, they were always deemed as "necessary" or "convenient" for organizational risk management purposes.

The CEO set about making immediate changes to improve the customer experience while still maintaining an appropriate level of risk management. He selected a small group of employees to meet with him the day after they all returned from their off-site meeting, examined the necessity of the policies, and was able to initiate revised policies that improved the customers' experience (e.g., reduced customer wait time) while empowering certain employees with more authority. Appropriate risk controls for the firm were maintained.

2. *Processes must be in sync with the organization's service vision.* If the service vision is about "customer comfort," then every process must be crafted to facilitate "customer comfort." Processes must also always defer to the organization's core values and service standards. Values and standards take precedence over processes and procedures. The organization's service vision, values, and standards should serve as filters that processes are tested against to ensure they are aligned with what is most important to the organization. If speed of service delivery is a key customer loyalty driver and is reflected in the service vision and a standard, then the organization's processes need to stand up to a test of "speed of service," using the customers' definition of speed.

3. *Processes must facilitate great internal service, not just great external service.* The creation of "silos" and shaky hand-offs between internal departments hurt process "morale." Silos can be real or just an attitude. In either case, they are a barrier to great service because they prevent the smooth transition of customers (internal and external) and/or issues that impact customers between steps in a process. In the case of a tie, external service trumps internal service. In other words, when designing a new process (or reviewing a process for alignment), the needs and perceptions of the external customer should be viewed as a priority over the desires for ease and efficiency of the internal customer.

4. *Process changes driven by "economics" must be scrutinized for their impact on customers before an accurate return on investment can be determined.* Too often, organizations evaluate the economics of process change solely on the "return on investment" in the process change itself without attaching value to the impact the change may have on customers. This is especially true if the impact on customer loyalty will most likely be negative. For example, enterprise resource planning

(ERP) initiatives too often are evaluated almost entirely on the basis of the cost of technology and change management without a careful analysis of their impact on customer loyalty. The result is a loud cry from customers about substandard service *after implementation*, which unfortunately causes customer loyalty to drop.

5. *Processes must be regularly updated to ensure they reflect customers' ever-changing expectations for service.* The top ten most important processes—those deemed to have the biggest impact on driving and sustaining customer loyalty—must be singled out annually for an "alignment check" and tune up. Today, customer expectations change at supersonic speed as customers are influenced by their service experiences with organizations of every type and effectiveness. Staying in touch with these ever-changing customer service expectations is crucial to an organization's success. Just as you would expect a complete checkup from your doctor during an annual physical, so too should your most important processes undergo the rigors of an annual evaluation of their effectiveness at delivering or enabling service to customers in an appropriate fashion.

6. *Processes that cease to achieve their purpose must be eliminated before their continued presence fools someone into thinking they are needed and they begin to fall under "special protection" by their custodian.* Processes that have been in place for an extended period tend to become overly respected and can become thought of as "untouchable." We are reminded of a client that failed to pay attention to how difficult it was for customers to connect with employees in their organization by telephone until one day they were jolted into awareness by a potentially very large referral source for new business. To our client's horror, the potential source described his ridiculously complex journey through an antiquated voice response unit (VRU) and shared his complete frustration in being unable to find a way through the maze to a real person. The organization immediately gathered a group of senior leaders and took them on a similar journey via speakerphone. Their embarrassment and irritation grew as they played the role of customer and became increasingly frustrated at the

hurdles they had created for their customers in trying to reach their very talented employees. The VRU programming, which had been effective when implemented, had grown stale and had become a very large irritant to customers. An annual "checkup" and "realignment" of processes could have prevented this situation.

7. *Processes are never completely "happy" unless they are employee friendly.* Leaders are responsible for the "morale" of processes, not the processes' custodian or owner. Research has shown that engaged and loyal employees are needed to drive the type of service that produces loyal customers. Just as you would use filters to ensure processes reflect the organization's service vision, so too should you use employee engagement as a "filter" for testing a process's impact on the employees who are affected by it. We know that executive leaders closely monitor an organization's customer service dashboard for indications of fluctuations in customer loyalty. They also must review customer intelligence for evidence of fluctuations in the alignment of processes. When the intelligence indicates the need for a process review or redesign, it is senior leadership's responsibility to implement such an initiative. The process owner's role is to ensure the process is working exactly as designed. Often, process custodians will sense the first signs of "unhappiness" in a process because they are so close to daily operations. They may sound the alarm of a process entering the realm of misalignment, but it is senior leadership's responsibility to ensure any adjustments necessary for realignment are in fact realized. If process "morale" is left to the process custodians, their closeness to the process will often prevent them from seeing that change is required.

The secret to maintaining processes in a state of "happiness" is to remember they are means, not ends. They are the ultimate servant in the quest for customer loyalty and devotion. Treating them as a common slave will only result in process acquiescence and, ultimately, customer disdain. But treating them as a contributing partner will yield process alignment and customer devotion.

Ten Steps to Creating Happy Processes

1. Determine the most critical business practices, processes, systems, and policies based on the significance of their impact on employee quality of work life, customer loyalty, and/or profitability.

2. Identify key alignment filters (key customer loyalty drivers, the service vision, standards and norms, critical strategic building blocks, etc.) to use in testing the critical business practices to determine which ones are out of alignment.

3. Using these alignment filters, develop a list of processes that need adjustment to become realigned.

4. Make sure the "realignment list" is all encompassing by comparing it to five service or system breakdowns you were involved in or know of over the past twenty-four months. What company-wide business practices, processes, systems, procedures, and policies, in place at the time, were ineffective at preventing these breakdowns? Review to make sure all are on your realignment list.

5. Develop criteria for prioritizing the list of "out of alignment" business practices, processes, systems, procedures, and policies. Consider criteria such as quick wins, "can't wait," major customer impact, and major employee impact to identify the top ten priorities to work on first.

6. Compare the top ten priorities to a list of exclusion criteria (e.g., "don't have the resources this year," "already being worked on," "have to wait for the new ERP system implementation") to determine which priorities need to come off the list.

7. Identify alignment project executive sponsors, an alignment project leader, and an alignment project "steering committee" to provide guidance, direction, and resources and to eliminate barriers to success.

8. Assign project team members and develop project plans.

9. Communicate, communicate, communicate about the project, progress, and plans.

10. Celebrate the milestone accomplishments and successes of the alignment project.

> Service systems that are low on the friendliness scale tend, by their very design, to subordinate convenience and ease of access for the customer in favor of the convenience of the people within the system.
>
> —Karl Albrecht
> co-author of *Service America in the New Economy*

13

Measure and Manage from the Customer's Point of View

The four most important words in service quality are: measure, measure, measure, and measure.

—Ken Dagley
President, Australian Customer
Service Association

Regardless of the business you are in and the size of your operation, measure you must! A commitment to service quality without a commitment to standards and measurement is a dedication to lip service, not customer service. Standards and measurement are critical to the smooth functioning—and improvement—of your service delivery system. While measurements come in many forms and serve different purposes, all share the same goal—creating a trusted guidance system for managers' decision making.

A common denominator among companies with reputations for high-quality service is their bias for setting service standards and their prodigious efforts to measure how well those standards are met. In complex service delivery systems—like those of United Parcel Service, Enterprise Rent-a-Car, or Southwest Airlines—that effort involves hundreds of standards and a multitude of measurement systems to keep service delivery on an even keel. In a simpler system, like that of a Chick-fil-A restaurant or the FedEx Kinko's Copies down on the corner, it takes far fewer standards and measures to keep on top of the "How are we doing?" question.

The Look of Customer-Focused Measurement

Chances are pretty good that your company already measures a number of things about the service delivery systems you manage all or part of. Just the same, it is a good idea to stop, step back from your system for a moment, and ask yourself whether your current measurement is driven by customer parameters or internal technical specs. To make sure the former, not the latter, energizes your measurement efforts, use these three general criteria for auditing—and perhaps improving—the customer focus of your service delivery system.

1. *Your measurements should reflect your "purpose."* Nothing makes your service vision—your purpose—more real to your frontline employees than measuring what you're doing against customer-focused norms.

If your service promise is for "timely deliveries on all shipments" and your customers have told you that means "twenty-four-hour turnaround on all orders," measure that. But don't just look inside. You're not done until the customer has taken delivery, so be sure you also measure the customer's perception of whether or not orders are arriving "in a timely fashion." Even if you're dead solid certain that a customer's order came and went in twenty-four hours—and twenty-four hours is twice as good as your nearest competitor—if the customer doesn't "feel" that the order arrived in a timely fashion, the customer is right and you are wrong.

Remember: For the customer, *perception* is all there is!

How can you be 100 percent "on time" but wrong about being "timely"?

- First, the twenty-four-hour standard is *your* technical standard, not the customer's. To the customer, "timely" is a perception, not a measurement, as it is to you.
- Second, "timely" or "on time" to you typically means when the order goes out *your* door. To customers, those same words may well mean the time the order comes in *their* door, is on the shelf in *their* warehouse, or is in hand and ready for distribution or use in *their* system.

Not your problem? *Wrong!* If your customers believe there is a problem, there is a problem—whether you think it's real or not. And you'd better have a systematic way of finding out about it. Your measurement system has to tell you about the problems customers are perceiving, and as soon as possible, not just comfort you with statistics about your adherence to your own technical standards.

2. *Your measurements should measure customer quality, not just technical quality.* There is a vital difference between the two.

- *Technical quality* is the measurement of all the mechanical and procedural things that must go right if your system is to work effectively and efficiently. Technical quality measures are *internal* indicators of your delivery system's specification-driven performance.

  Think: Down time, order waiting time, order assembly time, back order volume, order turnaround time, shipments per hour, time per phone call, and similar measures.

- *Customer quality* is the performance of your service delivery system from the *customer's* point of view. It is the assembly of elements that are important to the customer, as judged by the customer. These are the elements that are directly observable by the customer and that most directly determine their satisfaction with your service delivery system.

  Think: Ease of contact, order correctness and completeness, timeliness of order arrival, courtesy and empathy toward people dealt with, look of the package upon arrival, understandability of the bill, and similar subjective impressions.

Technical quality measures are important to trouble spotting, problem solving, and the smooth and cost-effective functioning of the system. Customer quality measures are important to customer delight and retention and to system improvement and priority setting.

Measuring What Matters to Customers

Whether they're designed to gauge quantitative or qualitative service dimensions, your customer-focused measures are meaningless if they measure the wrong things. Make sure your survey questions assess the service factors that customers believe are essential to winning their loyalty, not performance areas that market researchers or line managers assume are critical to keeping them coming back for more.

In organizations with extensive telephone customer contact, for example, the two most common measurements of the delivery system are length of phone calls and number of rings before pickup. Yet, customers we've asked about contact with such companies seldom, if ever, mention either factor. They're more concerned about getting the information they need, having their problems solved (ideally during that first contact), and not being put on hold for hours or connected to the voice-mail system from hell.

In some companies, these two measures have been automated and computerized as an employee surveillance and evaluation system. The claim is that such measurement systems improve service. They do not. They *may* improve productivity, which may or may not be related, but service is *not* the point of such measurement systems. Authority and accountability are.

Not only do they not have the desired effect on customers, but they also don't do a thing to help the people charged with delivering customer service. We've yet to talk to a frontline service worker hooked up to one of these electronic stopwatch systems who didn't: (1) resent the obvious lack of trust and (2) learn to trick the system anyway in self-defense. (How? Easy: Watch the time and hang up in mid-sentence when the call starts to go too long. If and when the mystified—or disgruntled—customer calls back, apologize . . . and blame it on "equipment failure.")

Are we suggesting that you not measure "number of rings before answer" or "length of talk time with customer"? No. We are saying that these and similar measurements, valuable as they may be for managing costs and monitoring system capacity, are not necessarily helping you manage service quality as perceived by your customer. And that means they're not helping—and may well be hindering—your people as they try to directly improve customer satisfaction and directly build customer retention.

The Customer Service Dashboard

Think of the array of data available to help guide your staff's customer service performance as a "dashboard" of sorts. When driving a car, it's essential to keep your eyes on the road and use your senses to successfully navigate, but doing so while ignoring the fuel or temperature gauge is asking for trouble. Likewise, as a service manager, you rely on your eyes and ears to evaluate how your staff is performing, but leaning too heavily on qualitative or subjective measures can provide a skewed vision of service quality.

That's why it's important to create the right dashboard—the right kind and number of formal metrics—to successfully guide and improve service performance. Customer service metrics can take on a life of their own unless they are aligned with an organization's key business strategies, policies, processes, and systems. For example, when developing a list of metrics to be included on your dashboard, ask the question: Does the organization have clear service standards, policies, and procedures that promote partnership between and among units, not just good teamwork within units? Without any cross-unit service metrics, it's difficult to get an early warning on the emergence of "silo" thinking that can prevent the kind of seamless, easy-to-do-business with service delivery that creates loyal customers.

Every service dashboard should include four types of metrics:

• *Course metrics* assess whether the organization is "on course" or is pursuing the direction intended. Typical customer service course metrics might include quantitative measures like number of customers retained, customers' estimated lifetime value, or profit per customer. Qualitative course metrics might be anecdotal comments from customers that suggest progress ("you come highly recommended from a friend") or improvement ("your call center representatives seem more efficient and friendly").

• *Correction metrics* include tools to facilitate progress and maintain service effectiveness. These are the means by which an organization gains a deeper and more complete understanding of course metrics. Quantitative service correction metrics might include measuring customer retention by particular product line or customer segment, customer satisfaction scores by type of customer, length of customer relationship, or "share of wallet" by segment. Qualitative correction metrics are things like types of customer complaints, types of errors that trigger refunds, or reasons customers give for leaving. Identifying the right *correction* metric starts with a dissection of the *course* metric. For example, if a key course metric is the number of customers under age twenty-five who re-enroll in a program after one year, the correction metrics might be derived from interviews with those who stay versus those who leave to determine major reasons for both.

• *Caution metrics* provide intelligence needed to shape or change strategic direction and keep pace with shifting customer needs. These data are vital to effective early warnings. Quantitative caution metrics might be those associated with long-range demographic variations, industry projections, and anticipated psychographic changes in a target customer population. Qualitative caution metrics could be results from focus groups, pilot tests, and futuring studies.

- *Context metrics* are tools to better understand the marketplace and how your business unit or organization compares relative to that environment. These metrics paint a picture of the setting in which the organization is operating at a given point in time and help to ensure you don't become so myopic or inwardly focused that competitive mistakes are made. Quantitative context metrics include how other similar organizations are faring in the same market conditions—data like same store customer churn compared to competitors or industry standing in revenue per employee. Qualitative metrics are things like how often the company is favorably mentioned in trade journal or business magazine articles, rankings in independent surveys, or recognition from your industry or profession.

As a supervisor or first-line manager, you may not have a lot of control over what gets measured and how it gets measured. But by thinking through what your current measurement does and does not give you, and how you are and are not using the results, you can affect the performance of your delivery system. And if you're not getting the kind of data you need—or are getting too much of the wrong kind of data—it's in your interest to build a case with the keepers of the measurement flame for changing this unproductive state of affairs. And the sooner the better!

Don't Try to Drive a Nail with a B Flat

Measurability is a valuable tool in monitoring service excellence. But if myopically seized upon, it can also be a time-wasting, cover-your-backside, proof-seeking effort. As research guru Michael Patton advised, "Anything not worth measuring is not worth measuring well."

The need to balance both bottom-line and life-line reasons for increasing customer loyalty led me to one of my favorite books, *Sea of Cortez*, written by John Steinbeck and Edward Ricketts in 1941. In one passage, the authors describe catching the fighter fish, the Mexican Sierra. Having fished for

Sierra in the exact same waters off the coast of Cabo San Lucas on the Southern tip of the Baja Peninsula, I can attest to the accuracy of his description. As you read the passage that follows, consider what it communicates about the implication of "metrics without methods."

> The Mexican Sierra has 17 plus 15 plus nine spines in the dorsal fin. These can easily be counted. But if the Sierra strikes hard on the line so that our hands are burned, if the fish sounds and nearly escapes and finally comes in over the rail, his colors pulsing and his tail beating in the air, a whole new relational externality has come into being—an entity which is more than the sum of the fish plus the fisherman.

> The only way to count the spines of the Sierra unaffected by this second relational reality is to sit in a laboratory, open an evil-smelling jar, remove a stiff colorless fish from the formalin solution, count the spines and write the truth. . . . There you have recorded a reality which cannot be assailed— probably the *least* important reality concerning either the fish or yourself.

There are no easy answers to measuring customer loyalty— especially in a fashion that demonstrates convincing cause and effect, not just correlation. Spend a million bucks adding a branch, and you can project the return. But, spend a like amount on enhancing a customer experience, and the concrete, irrefutable proof gets less precise.

Successful customer partnerships cannot be effectively measured with the same tools you might use to measure the financial impact of a merger or new computer. Using economic tools to measure the relational aspects of service quality is a bit like trying to drive a nail with a B flat. There is nothing wrong with B flats. They served Mozart well. But, when he had a hankering for carpentry, he chose a different tool.

Or as Marilyn Ferguson wrote in her book, *The Aquarian Conspiracy*, "In our lives and in our cultural institutions we have been poking at qualities with tools designed to detect quantities. By what yardstick do you measure a shadow, a candle flame? What does an intelligence test measure? Where in the medical armamentarium is the will to live? How big is an intention? How heavy is grief; how deep is love."

> 'Tain't nowhere near right, but it's approximately correct.
>
> —Howland Owl
> (Pogo's Quality Guru, explaining the inbred weaknesses of all measurement systems)

14

Serving Online: When Clicks Replace Bricks

The Internet is becoming the town square for the global village of tomorrow.

—Bill Gates

The word "wireless" is defined as the transfer of information without the use of electrical conductors. In many ways, this definition captures the blessing and the bother of Internet service. The mobility, speed, and ease of the Internet as a tool for "interlogue" are clearly worthwhile assets. However, robbed of the capacity to read nonverbal information, there is great potential for misinformation and misinterpretation. Without accurate dialogue, understanding can suffer.

One study at the University of California, Los Angeles indicated that up to 93 percent of communication effectiveness is determined by nonverbal cues.[23] Another study found that the impact of a performance was determined in 7 percent of cases by the words used, 38 percent by voice quality, and 55 percent by the nonverbal communication.[24] Stripping the lion's share of the effectiveness features from communications with customers puts enormous burden on those factors that are left.

The Internet is a lot like a rattlesnake. Rattlesnakes are not aggressive snakes until threatened. Then they provide a warning to their opponent in the form of an unmistakable rattle. But if the rattle is ignored, they strike quickly and with a bite laced with venom that has a lasting impact on the strikee. Successful organizations serving the online customer must be great "listeners for the rattle," intently monitoring all channels simultaneously. Once a rattle is heard from customers, the service provider must be prepared to react quickly, succinctly, and effectively.

Be Flexible

In today's cyber world, the diversity of service is loudly amplified. Brick-and-mortar service largely restricts access to those customers geographically nearby. Rarely do customers drive many miles to patronize a particular store or service. Consequently, customers of brick-and-mortar commerce hail from similar neighborhoods with similar values and mores. With Internet service accessible to all, no matter their demography, geography, or ethnology, organizations with too many rules and restrictions and frontline employees with too little decision-making authority can box service providers into responding with what customers perceive as stubbornness.

Flexibility is not just an attitude at the opposite end of rigidity; it emanates from a keen understanding of the customer and a desire to adapt the offering to fit the customer. We were working with the call center of a major utility that had elected to eliminate a segment of twenty-four/seven access to the call center for customers, forcing Sunday afternoon callers to wait until Monday morning. Their rationale was as follows: Only a handful of customers ever called then, so why worry? It seemed not to occur to them that they could have easily and inexpensively outsourced that service to a retired call center rep willing to cover the segment from home on Sunday afternoon. The cost of adding to the Monday morning handle time could have easily funded the part-time call center rep.

Customer segments are different in terms of their Internet preference. Convergys research revealed that millennials showed less preference for live phone support, whereas baby boomers showed increased preference. Their preference was driven in part by their growing frustration with automated phone systems. Generation X customers indicated they were not using live Web chat, e-mail, or automated phone systems as much as they would like. They relied more heavily on live phone support because the channels they really preferred either did not exist or were not being supported in the right way.[25]

The Convergys research also found a huge disconnect among millennials between what they were using and what they really wanted. Fifty-four percent of millennials said they have used or are likely to use texting for customer service; 47 percent have used or want to use social media for service; and 44 percent have used or want to use smart phone applications.[26]

Customers *do* expect a live Web chat to take longer than a live phone call, but if they knew it would take twice as long, 90 percent would opt to speak with a customer service rep.[27] There is no gain in providing live Web chats if the customer spends twenty minutes chatting with an agent and then decides to pick up the phone and spend ten minutes talking to another agent.

Be Inclusive

Buy a book from Amazon.com once or rent a movie on Netflix once and on your next visit to their site, the computer will suggest other books or movies you might like. "Customers assume that when they make a purchase, the record of that purchase will be readily available regardless of the channel it came from. All systems have to be synchronized," notes best-selling author Robert Spector.[28] Take a look at how many online companies have gone to "My" as the prefix for their personalization—MyFedEx, MyOfficeDepot, and the like.

All of us take that customerization dimension to be table stakes today. We have been taught by Internet providers to expect that they will remember us from previous encounters, know our history, recognize our IP address, and populate screens quickly when we transit from online to Web chat to live chat. We assume there will always be a trap door giving us easy access to a real person. Log on to landsend.com and the bottom left side of the home page offers an 800 number, a chat online, or a button to click for "call me." The "all about me" customer expects to be included in ways beyond, "Would you like to complete a survey at the end of this transaction?"

Service providers are answering that expectation with enormous creativity. For example, according to a blog on www.1to1media.com:

> High-tech networking giant Cisco recently tested the power of social media outlets with the launch of myPlanNet, a downloadable video game that allows players to assume the role of a CEO and solve business challenges using Cisco products. Although introduced using traditional live events, myPlanNet quickly gained widespread appeal among IT professionals who turned the simulation game into a B2B social media juggernaut spanning various channels worldwide. According to Cisco, the award-winning social media campaign for myPlanNet has been downloaded more than 35,000 times and has attracted more than 55,000 fans on its Facebook page.[29]

As Cisco and other innovative service providers know, collaboration is the core of partnership. Threadless.com invites their website community to vote on the coolest t-shirts designed by fellow amateurs. The winning entries become their product offerings, providing great exposure for budding designers and a sense of ownership by the community. Jackdaniels.com has a fan club called the Tennessee Squire Association. They asked squires in Texas to vote online for their favorite color (red, white, or blue) for the Jack Daniel's–sponsored race car to be run in the annual Texas 500 race. Mountain Dew created a user-generated movement to launch a new product. The process (called Dewmocracy) involved more than three million customers in various phases of the design, development, and marketing of a new drink ultimately called White Out.[30] Kodak has a digital media team including a chief blogger; a chief listener; more than a dozen full-time staffers who cover the Web, search engine optimization, and social media; and a network of part-time bloggers and tweeters around the world who represent different departments of the company.[31]

eBay is another great example of an organization that views customers as partners. Every sixty days, they invite twelve eBay users to journey to San Jose, California, to participate in the company's "Voice of the Customer" program. These select people visit almost every department to talk about ways to improve service. This focus group methodology goes one step further. Every month thereafter for six months, these same users are reassembled to explore emerging issues. As users evolve from being interviewees to feeling like members of the organization, they get bolder in their input. They may come in as a "customer with a concern," but they leave as a "partner with a plan." The byproduct of these customer conversations has been important new offerings (like iPhone apps) and unique service enhancements for eBay.

eBay CEO John Donahoe put it this way: ". . . we were not as outside-in as we needed to be. Consumers are driving a lot of change and we've found ourselves better off if we learn how to take advantage of them. . . . The passion our sellers feel is a blessing. The minute they stop caring and screaming is the minute we should be concerned. We've tried to be much more genuine and authentic about listening to their feedback."[32]

Be Honest

The Internet world, being devoid of many of the usual signals we rely on to sense deception, demands absolute and complete honesty. It requires the pinnacle of transparency. Log on to Bill Marriott's blog "Marriott on the Move," and you will learn about the new Marriott extended-stay ExecuStay corporate apartment brand. You get a detailed, up close and personal tour of a typical apartment.[33] Marriott is a "people first" culture that places honesty as a centerpiece of the "home-like work atmosphere" they nurture. Walmart.com puts customer reviews right beside all the products they feature on their home page.

The truth-seeking component of effective partnership is that which values candor and openness. It is the dimension that honors authenticity and realness. The path to honesty in relationships is paved with risk taking. It involves the courage to ask for feedback as well as the commitment to value it in a way that is affirming to the sender. Honesty may sometimes leave relationships temporarily uncomfortable and bruised, but truth always leaves the partnership hearty and healthy. It exterminates guilt and deceit and ennobles wholesomeness and trustworthiness.

At its core, partnering is a commitment to a conversation with customers rather than unilateral action. If decision making is made without customer input, it corrupts the service covenant. Partnering starts with asking for input. It continues with enlisting others in problem resolution rather than positioning yourself as the sole "answer person." Partnering is operating with the faith that wisdom lies within us all and that by tapping the collective brainpower of customers and associates, the organization is stronger, more responsive, and more adaptive to the ever-changing requirements of customers and employees.

Honesty is the byproduct of great conversations. Effective Internet servers nurture a vibrant community and foster listening posts. The more the Internet feels like a cyber watering hole, friendly to all as well as protector of all, the more it becomes a crucible of trust and an assembly of importance. It starts to resemble the old-fashioned marketplace where farmers brought produce to sell to merchants and consumers relied on the confidence derived from dependability. As on the Internet marketplace at its best, rotten apples were banned, and devious bargain hunters were disdained. Someone just passing through town might get away with a shady deal, but returning vendors were required to be trustworthy.

Be Fair

One feature the Internet world lacks that face-to-face commerce typically contains is a tactile connection. Walk into a store to buy a new pair of shoes and you can feel the leather and the fit. Buy the same item online and, unless you are repurchasing an article that worked before, there is a risk that what you see will not match what you need. This makes fairness a much more crucial feature of the service covenant.

One of our clients happens to be the largest wholesale auto auction company in the country. Buyers and sellers come together at the auto version of the "farmer's market." Major rental car companies are there to unload last year's models, auto manufacturers are there to deplete glutted inventory of a model that undersold projections, and banks are there to sell leased or repossessed vehicles. Used-car dealers are there as buyers of fresh inventory for their lots. If there is a dispute over a purchased vehicle that was not as promised ("There was frame damage your inspector totally missed!"), arbitration is on site to resolve buyer–seller disputes.

When the company elected to provide a portal that would enable buyers to watch auctions online and bid along with buyers on site, the importance of full disclosure and fair dealings ratcheted up dramatically. All vehicles sold had a "condition report" (CR) that provided buyers with details about the vehicle before the auction. Online buyers began asking for more close-up photos of the scratch mentioned in the CR, or a notation in the CR indicated that the inside of the vehicle revealed the previous owner smoked cigars—all elements the person on site could see, touch, feel, or smell.

However, the greatest change between online and in-lane buyers was the standards for arbitration. The old rules failed to take into account that the online buyer was making a purchase with only "at-a-distance" sight as their primary tool for gauging worth. To level the playing field, the company instituted a "we'll buy it back" policy if the buyer registered any displeasure with the fairness of the deal within the first thirty days after purchase.

The future of online commerce is beacon bright. Forrester Research projects that e-commerce sales in the United States will grow at a 10 percent compound annual growth rate through the next four years.[34]

The warp speed and surprise power of the Internet means that the best antidote to the bite of a wired customer intent on striking is to be a fast fixer and a sincere healer, not a sounding board. That means asking customers for their definition of fair and then adding to it. It means drawing the customer in as a source for learning, not reaching for the checkbook in hopes they will go away. The bottom line is that the Internet customer should be thought of as a partner who, because of his or her access to many cyber villages, can be a valued scout, interpreter, and peacemaker.

Value in the Village

Social media, such as blogs, Facebook, Twitter, Pinterest, Digg, and Yelp, provide concrete evidence that customers are changing the way they define marketplace. In some ways the Internet is a return to the old-fashioned village. While the new village is a global community, it nevertheless has many of the features of the village of yesteryear. In a small town, merchants knew you and catered to your specific needs. They acted on history and patterns of previous purchases. They'd even open the store after hours if you needed something. Over the last fifty years, commerce has become distant, impersonal, and one size fits all as the service covenant has altered. The Internet in general and social media in particular have helped connect customers with businesses in ways that are more personalized, open, around the clock, and valued.

Another feature of the old-fashioned village was generosity. The village is where the concept of "the baker's dozen" originated. Kids got a free taste at the candy shop; merchants gave away "secret recipes," and adults got a "take it home and try it" assurance behind products. There was no need for a written "money-back guarantee"—the merchant *was* the guarantee. The closeness of shared space required varied means to maintain relationship balance. Customers and merchants relied on neighborly practices. A spirit of abundance was a way to start and maintain valuable relationships.

Like the old-fashioned village, the Internet is a world under a microscope. Value must be real and look real. The eye candy of websites must be interesting, easy, fast, and imaginative, or the cyber traveler will only be a drive-by window shopper or a targeted bargain hunter with little intent of sticking around (called being sticky) or coming back. It makes generosity—providing *extra* to value, not thinking of value as *tit for tat*—an important means to ensure a genuine partnership.

Log on to Gerbers.com, and their homepage is organized by the stages of a baby's life, from pregnancy to preschool. Not only are site visitors given product information relevant to a specific stage, but Gerber also provides information on growth and development, nutrition, and feeding and offers parental advice. Intuit gives visitors smart advice by product and links them to a community of Intuit product users.

Internet is a word we repeat without thinking much about its real meaning. When we shorten the word to *Net*, we remove the most important part. *Inter* means "between," as in interchange, interconnect, interface, interact, interdependence, and interpersonal. It implies mutuality and reciprocity, a give and take that respects both ends of a promise waiting to be kept. It can be the shining manifestation of partnership at its finest. And, it can transform a customer ready to take a nastygram viral into one eager to spread "likes" to all friends and family.

> In the physical world an unhappy customers tells six friends; in the cyber world an unhappy customer tells six thousand.
>
> —Jeff Bezos
> CEO and Founder of Amazon

15

Add Magic: Creating the Unpredictable and Unique

He who gives great service gets great returns.
—Elbert Hubbard
Nineteenth-century American writer

Great systems, well-designed and managed, start with a simple goal: reliability—delivering on your *core promise* to the customer. An airline that promises to take you from New York to Minneapolis, but deposits you in Indianapolis instead, does not make you a happy traveler, no matter how friendly the cabin crew or how smooth the ride.

But that's just for starters. How do you compete for customers when you are one of three airlines, each boasting five flights a day between New York and Minneapolis, all of which deliver passengers to the right "apolis" safely, on time, and with most of their luggage in hand?

Taking off and landing uneventfully will make you just one of three carriers that meet the basic core requirements of air transportation. To distinguish yourself in highly competitive, "me-too" markets, your systems will need to help you reliably and consistently offer something "extra" that draws business away from your competitors. We call the extra dimension that creates indelible customer memories *service magic.*

Adding Magic

Service magic, much like stage magic, is not simply serendipity or a fluke but a set of learned skills developed through desire and mastered through planning, practice, and a keen understanding of the customer psyche. In a nutshell, service magic is about creating memorable surprises for customers who have come to expect the bland, indifferent customer service that characterizes so many transactions in today's business world.

What service magic *is not* is value-added service as most of us know it. Ask customers what actions they consider value added and they will focus on taking the expected experience to the next step—"they gave me more than I anticipated." Value-added is a predictable linear response—the upgrade, the complimentary dessert, or the discount coupon for the next visit. It has its own importance and place in the service experience, as we'll explore later in the chapter. Service magic, on the other hand, is unpredictable and unique. When you are left thinking, "I wouldn't have thought of that," you have probably witnessed service magic. We like to think of it as service with imagination more than service with generosity.

Consider this situation: A customer traded in an older model car for a new one. A week after owning the car, she turned on the radio for the first time to discover the dealership had programmed the radio stations from her old car's radio into the new one. That bit of unexpected personalization created a small thrill of magic for the customer.

Francie Johnsen is a part-time CVS pharmacist in Dallas and is famous for service magic. The whole store sparkles when Francie shows up. Before Francie, should you have a prescription called in or dropped off for later retrieval, you got a mechanical "someone in this household has a prescription ready for pickup" message on the answering machine. She put a stop to that. When the vet called in a prescription for our cat, the answering machine at our house played an even more personalized message: "Taco, meow, meow," the message pronounced with Francie's voice, "Tell your parents, meow, meow, that your prescription is ready, meow, meow!" Not only did she call the cat, she spoke fluent kitty! That's service magic at its finest!

The power of such thoughtful, beyond-the-norm actions lies in their uniqueness. A steady diet of such extravagance and not only can you abuse the bottom line, but you also risk turning the unique into the usual . . . and the magic vanishes. The trick is to teach your staff how to pick its spots and seek out the small magical touches that, by virtue of their novelty, have a disproportionately large impact on customer memories.

Using Preplanned Value-Addeds

While service magic is the gold standard of customer delight, the preplanned value-added is a close runner up in terms of fostering customer loyalty. Used wisely, such tools are an effective complement to magical interludes.

The frequent-customer programs developed as value-addeds by airlines, hotels, car rental companies, and even department stores and grocery stores are clearly preplanned. But such orchestrated "extras" don't have to predictable or bland, as guests of the Hotel Monaco in downtown Chicago will gladly tell you. First-time visitors checking in to the hotel usually do a double take when the front desk clerk gives them a room key, offers directions to their room, and then hands them a goldfish. In a bowl. For companionship.

For the confused—and who wouldn't be?—the desk person explains, "We're a pet-friendly hotel. Since you don't have a pet with you, we'd be pleased to loan you one of ours." The piscatorial value-added has gone over so big that many repeat guests ask for a specific fish—by name. The goldfish is only the opening salvo in the Hotel Monaco's attempts to impress with preplanned extras. In-room mini-bars have a complement of fun little "just because" items, such as wax lips, yo-yos, candy necklaces, Silly Putty, and Etch-a-Sketch boards. Turn-down service offers surprises as well. One night there might be a Tootsie Roll on the pillow, the next a pack of Pixie Stix or, if guests are lucky, the occasional Illinois state lottery ticket.

Make Service a Big Boy Event

There are two things I remember about my very first suit. It was a powder blue suit—perfect for Easter Sunday church. And, it was a "big boy" event. I was seven years old. The store was a two-hour drive from my rural home town and was visited only every August to buy school clothes. But this purchase required a special spring journey.

The "big boy" event started with the sales person pulling up a chair to sit in front of me at my eye level. He shook my hand and introduced himself by his first name, not "Mr." Without a single glance at my dad, he asked me about my favorite color and my second favorite color. He asked me about my hobbies and my best friend's name. We were pals in a matter of minutes. I walked out of the store very tall with a suit in my favorite color, a white dress shirt, a pair of shoes, and a tie in my second favorite color. Did I mention that I was seven?

Magic service can be simply creating a relationship laced with profound respect. Respect is more than admiration; it is confident deference, a willingness to elevate and affirm. And, as customers, when we get obvious respect, we never forget the feeling.

Eight Times to Include Value-Addeds

1. *For the Good, Solid, Steady, No-Complaints, No-Noise Customer.* Unspectacular, uncomplaining, salt-of-the-earth customers are often the most neglected. It's easy to take them for granted. It isn't easy to replace them with similarly good-natured people. If you do business with North Carolina–based Wilson Fence Company, expect to receive a letter beginning, "All too often, we do business with nice people, such as yourself, and then go on as if nothing had ever happened or without giving the customer a second thought. We would like to take a few minutes out of a busy day to personally thank you for your business."

2. *For the Customer Who Has Done You the Favor of Complaining.* By bringing a real or potential problem to your

attention, complaining customers are giving you a chance (1) to regain their loyalty and goodwill, and (2) to spot and fix problem areas in your service system that other customers might suffer through in silence. We know one CEO of a hotel chain who sends a personal "Thank you for bringing it to my attention" note to any customer who complains via comment card, letter, or phone call.

3. *For a New Customer Who Has Just Placed a Second Order or Increased the Level of Business they are Doing with You.* One printing company we've worked with doesn't take new business as its due. New customers receive a special information packet, hand-delivered by the store manager, along with a gift jar (embossed with the company's address and phone number, of course!) filled with candy. Is yours empty? Let 'em know—they'll refill it when they deliver your next printing job.

4. *For a Customer Who Has Thanked You.* When someone goes out of their way to express their gratitude for something you've done in the course of your business relationship with them, you have a tremendous opportunity to deepen and strengthen the bond by responding in kind. A good friend wrote to Ralston-Purina to let the company know just how much her cat enjoyed Purina Cat Chow—Tabby wouldn't even touch other brands and would actually pick out the Purina pieces and leave the rest if her owner tried to mix two together. A few weeks after writing, the cat owner received a thank-you note and a coupon. She was surprised, but she shouldn't have been.

5. *For a Customer Who Has Been Through a Difficult Time.* When things don't go smoothly, but your customer hangs in there with you, or when a loyal customer has learned the true meaning of Murphy's Law, a little "something for nothing" and corporate TLC is clearly in order. A woman who regularly shopped at Stew Leonard's Connecticut dairy store went home empty handed one evening when the computerized cash registers crashed. She couldn't wait for the system to come back online because that evening was her husband's birthday, a fact she shared with a store manager when she

called to offload a little frustration. In short order, a Stew Leonard's station wagon pulled up outside her home with her groceries and a cake with the frosted greeting "Happy Birthday from Stew and the Gang."

6. *When Going Out of Your Way Will Prevent a Customer from Having a Problem.* Consider the Hairy Cactus Nail Salon in Cincinnati, Ohio, a full-service salon that also provides manicure services. Understanding that time is money and that many women have ruined their not-quite-dry nails immediately upon leaving the salon, the Hairy Cactus came up with a simple but creative solution. Employees take the customer's purse and keys, open the salon door, escort her to her car, open the car door, put her belongings securely in the car, start the car, assist her into the seat, and then watch her go safely on her way with not a chip or smudge to be seen.[35]

7. *For a Good Customer Who Has the Potential for Bringing You New Customers or Increased Business.* Word-of-mouth advertising is more persuasive than any other kind. It's absolutely permissible to put words in the mouths of customers whose endorsement of your services can serve as a significant professional reference for your business. Adding a free car wash to a tune-up for Mr. Jones makes good sense for the local Flying Flivver dealership—especially if Mr. Jones is the purchasing manager for ABC Widgets and the person who buys ABC's company cars.

8. *Anyone for Whom You Feel Like Doing a "Good Deed."* Sometimes giving a little value-added service just makes you feel good, regardless of whether or not it directly affects future business. A customer of Umpqua Bank in his mid-seventies stopped by the nearest branch to request a stop payment on a check he had written to a firewood supplier. The supplier had promised to deliver a load of firewood and split it. The firewood was delivered but the supplier claimed he didn't have time to split it! "Go get an ax!" was the solution the supplier offered when the elderly man asked how he was to get the wood split. The bank retail service manager had to inform the customer that, unfortunately, his check to the supplier had already been deposited.

For most banks that would have been the end of the story. But, that's not how the "World's Greatest Bank" does customer service! With two other associates, axes in hand, the retail service manager drove eighty miles to the customer's home. They split and stacked the wood and swept the garage clean! You can imagine the emotional impact on the customer who's only source of heating was his fireplace. How many times do you think the Umpqua customer has repeated his firewood story?

> We view "Going the Extra Mile" service as an honor—not an obligation.
>
> —Hal Stringer
> President, Peerless Systems, Inc.

16

Make Recovery a Point of Pride

The true test of an organization's commitment to service quality isn't the stylishness of the pledge it makes in its marketing literature, it is the way the organization responds when things go wrong for the customer.

—Ron Zemke
Father of Knock Your Socks Off Service

All around the country, frontline service people have to deal with customers who experience service failure. It's not their fault, anymore than it's the customers' (although it's worth pointing out that about 30 percent of all problems with products and services are indeed *caused* by customers).

No service system is or ever will be 100 percent perfect. Sooner or later, something will go wrong. When it does, how your front line responds can not only make the best of a bad situation, but it can actually turn disappointment into customer satisfaction—sometimes even into customer delight! Hence the term *recovery*.

Recovery isn't simply about doing the right thing for your fellow human beings—it also can add dollars to your bottom line. A series of studies by TARP Worldwide found that when aggrieved customers had their problems satisfactorily resolved in quick fashion, they were more likely to purchase additional products than even those customers who experienced no problems with the organization to begin with. Research at Minneapolis-based National Car Rental found an 85 percent chance that a satisfied customer would rent again from National and a *90 percent* probability that a customer who experienced great service recovery would rent again.[36]

Home shopping service QVC Inc. understands how good recovery can help cement customer loyalty. A few years ago the company was selling NFL team rings at a record pace, primarily to wives buying them as Christmas gifts for husbands. But when QVC's guarantee to ship all rings before Christmas fizzled, the company knew it had to go beyond simply crediting customers for their purchases, as many other companies might have done. Resourceful employees remembered there were some high-quality NFL team jackets in the QVC warehouse, so the company matched them against ordered team rings and mailed them before Christmas—at no cost to customers.

Customer-centric organizations understand that solving customer problems swiftly and skillfully is more than a loss leader—it can contribute directly to revenue growth and profitability. At a minimum, good recovery is one of the best tools at your disposal for improving customer retention. The impact of poor recovery, on the other hand, goes far beyond the loss of a single customer. The salesperson or customer service rep who dismisses a complaining customer with an "I can't help you, that's our policy," positions the company to lose dozens, if not hundreds, of potential customers. As ample research over the past twenty years has shown, unhappy customers go out of their way to tell as many people as possible about their bad experience, and the potential audience for these tales of woe has grown exponentially with the advent of e-mail, online discussion boards, and blogs.

Recovery Defined

Service recovery includes all the actions your people take to get a disappointed customer back to a state of satisfaction. Like the hospital staff or doctor nursing a sick patient back to health, service recovery is returning the customer "back to normal."

But great service recovery does not happen by luck or solely through the interpersonal skills of your frontline people. Effective service recovery is planned and managed. It's a system that has to be designed and used just like any other system in your business. And your people have to know how to make it work on the customer's behalf. You may be asking yourself, "Is this service recovery stuff something we even need to talk about? Why not just put our energy into doing it right the first time? And, besides, maybe talking about mistakes will cause mistakes to happen more often—sort of a Pygmalion effect. Shouldn't our goal be zero defects? Shouldn't we accentuate the positive and eliminate the negative, as the old song used to advise?"

If service were always (or even mostly) perfect, we wouldn't need to talk about it. But it isn't. Service is neither designed nor delivered in a hermetically sealed room, where no contaminants can get into the process. It happens on the sales floor, in checkout lines, over the phone, on e-commerce sites, with the involvement of third parties, and subject to the disruptive influence of everything that is going on around it.

Instead of shuddering at the very mention of a potential problem, it's far better to prepare your people and the systems they work with to handle those occasional shortfalls. Keep in mind that customers have very different and unique requirements for "what is good service." A small mistake that causes one customer to say "ah, no problem" can make another customer livid.

Over the last twenty years, we've spent a lot of time researching the whys and wherefores of service recovery. Consistently, we find six caring actions that combine to make service recovery systematic, memorable, and satisfying.

1. *Apologize.* The point is not to determine who's to blame. It's to solve the problem. If your customers have a problem, chances are they're not happy. The first step to problem solving is to acknowledge the fact that—at least in the customers' eyes—a problem exists. As Tom Oliver, a senior vice president of sales and service at Federal Express once told us,

"If the customer believes he has a problem, he has a problem. Period." So, start by having your people tell them, personally and sincerely, "I'm sorry."

A 2005 "customer rage" study by the Customer Care Alliance of Alexandria, Virginia, found that only 25 percent of respondents with service problems heard "I'm sorry" from customer contact employees, while 59 percent said that's what they wanted to hear. And some 75 percent wanted an explanation of why the problem occurred, but only 18 percent received one.[37]

2. *Listen and empathize.* This is not the time to instruct customers in the finer points of what they should have done to avoid the problem in the first place. Customers resent being lectured to. What they mostly want your people to do right now is just listen. Listening and empathizing help customers unwind, get it out of their systems, and feel they're talking to someone who really cares about taking care of things.

3. *"Fair fix" the problem.* After listening (so they know exactly what's at issue), your people can snap to and, based on customer information and suggestions, work to resolve the problem. Usually, what customers want now is what they wanted originally—and the sooner the better. At Chick-fil-A restaurants, for example, if a customer arrives home to discover he was given the wrong drive-through order, an employee will personally travel to his residence to deliver the right one.[38]

4. *Offer atonement.* Your recovery system will earn high marks from customers if it includes, even symbolically, some form of atonement that, in a manner appropriate to the issue at hand, says, "I'd like to make it up to you." But atonement is more than simply the "it's on us" or "no charge" offer. The word symbolic is carefully chosen; it suggests that little acts of caring, when sincerely done, mean a lot to customers. Consider the atonement offered by Aurora Health Care of Milwaukee, Wisconsin, when a patient who'd just moved out of state discovered she was overcharged on a bill. Remembering that the woman complained about having to call long distance to correct "their" mistake, the hospital's

billing department included a complimentary phone card along with her refund check.[39]

Of course, the bigger the service breakdown—and the more valued the customer—the more impressive the atonement will have to be to restore aggrieved customers to a state of satisfaction.

5. *Keep your promises.* Recovery time is double jeopardy "where the stakes are doubled and the scores can really change." Your system has already failed once. If your people make promises they can't keep in trying to get your business back in the customer's good graces, it will be throwing gas on the fire. Employees need to know how to be realistic about what they can and can't deliver, and how quickly.

6. *Follow up.* In a few days, or a few weeks, have your people check back to make sure things really did work out to your customer's satisfaction. That kind of thoroughness and demonstrated concern builds loyalty that can weather future storms and helps set you apart from competitors.

Inside the Mind of an Aggrieved Customer

Once you have a recovery system in place, you have to factor in three important modifiers that govern the process from the customer's standpoint.

1. *Customers have expectations for how effective service recovery should happen.* Of course, you cannot learn what the customer expects unless and until you ask, which means soliciting complaints. There are solid data on the value of that orientation. Remember that only about one dissatisfied customer in twenty-five complains. Yet complaining customers can actually become more loyal than customers who pronounce themselves satisfied . . . if they've been listened to and responded to in a way that says you want them to come back again, despite this momentary glitch.

What does this mean to you as a manager? It means looking at customer feedback as a gift. When you get complaints from customers, share the information at the front line in a positive, not punitive, fashion. Rather than seek to find a guilty party, show your people that your objective is to retain the customer. If you shoot the messenger, your frontline people will neither encourage customer feedback nor report to you the service problems they identify. *You'll never find your fail points until it's too late.*

What's more, whenever you receive a complaint, you should see and hear not one whining malcontent but twenty-five valuable corporate assets assembled around your desk deciding whether they ever want to come back and do business with you again.

2. *When customers experience a service breakdown, they need to be fixed as well as their problems.* Relationships are built on trust. A bad experience with you hacks away at that trust and creates an expectation (actually, a dread) that the same thing will happen the *next* time, too. That's why you want your people to listen and empathize first, and only then begin to ask problem-resolution questions.

Make sure they know how to respond to the Smokescreen Principle. Complaining customers often start by throwing up an emotional, sometimes even irrational, smokescreen first to find out how serious you are about listening to them. If your people dismiss the ranting and raving out of hand as sheer exaggeration, they're missing the point. Customers aren't used to having someone listen when they complain. This is their way of testing how serious you are.

Understanding and sympathizing with a customer's emotional state when events veer far off their anticipated course are essential first steps to returning them to a state of satisfaction. It's at this point where right or wrong takes a back seat and when the customer's unique perspective on the problem must be heard, understood, and if at all possible, honored.

If you pass the test and get past that smokescreen, they will calm themselves down to the point that you finally unearth the rational, logical stuff that is key to fixing the problem. The emotional stuff is not going to help you fix the problem. But unless and until you get through it to the real issues, there's not much you can really accomplish.

3. *Effective planning leads to effective service recovery.* Top service providers identify places in their delivery system where service predictably fails and customers are left disappointed. Airlines and hotels often overbook, trains and planes experience weather delays or mechanical problems, restaurants overcook meals, and DVD rental companies mail the wrong movies to customers. Smart organizations outline service recovery standards to provide frontline people guidance in how to handle the customer who has been victimized. Although every situation is somewhat unique, guidance and clarity of expectations can provide frontline people the tools they need to come off competent and confident to the customer.

When it comes to service recovery, remember the axiom, *At that point where the customer is most insecure or incensed, you want your frontline people to be the most competent and confident.* The more you're able to work out the details of that approach in advance, the more recovery success you're likely to achieve.

Five Ways to Make Recovery Routine and Support Your People

1. *Eliminate barriers.* The more paperwork and policy your frontline people have to fill out, duplicate, circulate, and take care of, the less time they'll have to really listen to the customer and the longer it will take them to find solutions to problems that the customer will find satisfying.

2. *Train your people's response.* At no time will the listening and empathy skills of your frontline people be tested more than when they have to deal with an irate, dissatisfied customer. Give them training that helps them develop skills beyond simply smiling. They need to know how to listen, problem solve, and handle the stress of dealing with upset customers. It's vital to help them learn not to take things said or done by "customers from hell" personally and to encourage them to vent frustrations off stage, not in the heat of the moment when interacting with customers.

3. *Support and encourage.* Be quick to praise and slow to censure. As noted performance consultant Martin Broadwell said, "Frontline people need all the praise and encouragement you can give them. They get all the bullets anyone can take from the customers. Praise is the bulletproof vest. The supervisor has to be the one to give praise and give it generously."

4. *Separate praise and critique.* Nothing is more demoralizing to a frontline person than to have the boss say something like, "Pat, you did a nice job on that . . . *but* you should have remembered to . . . ." The compliment is always lost in the critique, diluting the value of both and tearing away a piece of the front liner's self-esteem. When it comes to recognition, make sure to "ban the buts."

5. *Always back your people in public.* When customers come to you with a complaint about a person on your staff, listen openly and nonjudgmentally, thank them for bringing it to your attention, but avoid a black-or-white determination based on "right and wrong." Find out what needs to happen to make the customer whole. Take care of that. Then, separately, calmly, and generally in private, meet with the frontline person involved. Treat mistakes as opportunities for problem solving and learning, not rebuke and punishment. Forgiveness fosters courage and builds faith that managerial support will be present in the face of the occasional error.

> When it comes to service recovery, there are three rules to keep in mind: (1) do it right the first time, (2) fix it properly if it ever fails, and (3) remember: there are no third chances.
>
> —Leonard Berry
> Marketing Professor,
> Texas A&M University

Imperative 5
Train and Coach

Learning is a way of life in Knock Your Socks Off Service companies. In the past, new employee training often consisted of nothing more than "watch John for a few hours, then I'll turn you loose on the customers." If employees made some little mistakes during their first few weeks, well, customers understood about breaking in new help.

That was then, and this is now.

Today, a walk-in-off-the-street, start-tomorrow-at-full-speed match is unlikely. Your methods, policies, and procedures are unique. So is the way you want customers treated. As for asking your customers to tolerate on-the-job training—forget that!

Knock Your Socks Off Service companies routinely spend the equivalent of 3 percent to 5 percent of salaries training employees—experienced as well as new. Managers believe that keeping everyone on top of changes in technology, competition, and customer demands is critical to success and survival.

Management support is equally critical to success in Knock Your Socks Off Service companies. Employees need to know and be able to see clear evidence that you are behind them in their efforts. They need to feel sure that you are on their side, that even if they make a mistake trying to do a good job for a customer, you will applaud the effort, if not the outcome.

Employees need to see themselves as colleagues, if not customers, in your eyes. Your personal credo should be, "If you're not serving the customer, you'd better be serving someone who is."

17

Start on Day One (When Their Hearts and Minds Are Malleable)

Coming together is a beginning. Keeping together is progress. Working together is success.

—Henry Ford

In the olden days of training, we used to talk about "getting them before they have teeth" —bringing on new people whose ideas and attitudes were open and unencumbered by a lot of bad habits and experiences.

- At that early stage of their job tenure, they were much more likely to accept our rationale for doing things in a certain way.
- If, however, we waited months, even years, before we started to try to build their Knock Your Socks Off Service skills, we often had the same kind of challenge orthodontists face when patients wait until they are adults before trying to do something about a gap-toothed grin.

137

Today we are committed to the importance of starting employees off with more than just the right technical skills. Marcia J. Hyatt, former director of employee development for CenterPoint Energy, a natural gas distribution firm, said it well when we first interviewed her on the topic. "If we believe employees treat customers the way they themselves are treated," she said, "then isn't it critical that we are as careful about the first impression we make on new employees as we expect them to be of the first impression they make on customers?"

If you believe, as we do, that actions often speak louder than words, then it is critical that we think about the entire new employee orientation *process* as carefully as we think about the basic program's content. Just as with our customers, we have to manage our people's initial experiences with the organization. Those first moments of truth on the new job can set the tone for years to come; they can, in fact, determine whether the new employee has a long tenure with the organization or will have packed and departed in short order and been replaced by another in an unending succession of slot fillers and seat warmers.

What message do we send to the new employees who report for the first day of a new job, only to find their supervisor and most of their new peer group absent, out of town, in meetings, or otherwise occupied? What values are we communicating when we drop them off in their new cubicle, e-mail them a hyperlink to the new employee manual on the company intranet site, and bury them with administrative and benefit forms?

The message isn't that the organization views them as a valuable resource—it's that they are simply the latest warm body to fill a seat and are to be moved as cost-efficiently as possible down the orientation assembly line. Yet plenty of research shows how effective good orientation can be at reducing avoidable turnover of new hires:

- Companies that provide a well-structured, comprehensive orientation can reduce turnover by up to 50 percent within two years, according to a study by Deliver the Promise, a consulting firm based in San Anselmo, California. The investment needed to build effective orientation programs pales in comparison to the high costs of turnover, the study found.

- A study at a large computer company demonstrated that the time for new people to reach full productivity shrank from five months to three months for employees who had been carefully oriented to the company in general and their job and department in particular.

Traditions

Perhaps the best-known example of turning the new employee orientation program into a sophisticated process with far-reaching consequences is the Traditions course at Disneyland and Walt Disney World. Every new employee who goes to work "at the park" is a graduate, whether they're going to be wearing badges that say *Guest Relations* or operating a broom and a dustbin.

The Traditions course is visible evidence of the extraordinary care that Disney takes to make sure that new employees understand the culture, values, and expectations of the organization. In the Disney vernacular, the world consists of only two classes of people: the "guests" who visit the park and the "cast members" who work there. In the Disney approach, new hires get a rare dose of reality as part of the new-employee orientation process. They're shown, in detail, how hot, tired, and cranky guests are capable of behaving—and misbehaving—and given an introduction to the ways the organization expects them to handle that important part of their job.

An equally far-reaching, although less obvious, part of the orientation of new cast members is the way they are treated during the orientation program—and indeed, the care with which the whole orientation process is structured. The Traditions program is carefully scripted and conducted in a comfortable, specially designed Traditions training room. Instructors are well aware that they are setting the tone for the way these new hosts and hostesses will treat guests when they make their first on-stage appearances. They're upbeat but realistic, supportive but challenging.

Other organizations combine special treatment for new hires with an early dose of service-related training. At some Fairmont Hotel and Resort properties, employees arriving for their first day on the job have their cars valet parked or receive vouchers for a free night's stay at a property. Others wear bathing suits during orientation to experience the spa's exfoliating showers and mineral baths. The on-boarding program, designed to help new hires experience what guests go through—and to make them feel like VIPs in those highly impressionable first days on the job—is a result of focus groups that identified "showing empathy" as a key way for Fairmont to separate itself from competitors.[40]

Tips for Making Orientation Work

What makes a first-rate new employee orientation program tick? Human resource and training managers say some of the best programs share these features:

1. *They avoid the day one "information dump."* The last thing people want on the first day of a new job, when excitement is at its peak, is to spend most of it filling out forms and reading benefit information. Shrewd companies have new employees complete these administrative tasks, as well as set up e-mail accounts and passwords, in advance of their first day. Rather than bury new hires in paperwork, they seek to maximize interaction with coworkers and bosses on day one, as well as familiarize them with the building layout. Some of the most successful orientation programs pair new employees with a "buddy" for the first few weeks to show them the ropes and help them begin building a social network.

Realizing that information overload is a real problem on day one—and that retention of content is often low due to nervousness or distractions—more companies are opting for a staggered approach to on-boarding. They hold a series of orientation meetings over the first month or two of a new hire's tenure to focus on different topics and give people more time to digest material and to develop greater breadth of understanding about the organization.

2. *They make orientation the joint responsibility of human resources (HR) and line managers.* Specifically, the most effective on-boarding programs maintain that HR should take responsibility for communicating information of organization-wide, relevant-to-all-new-employees nature, whereas supervisors should concentrate on issues unique to the employee's workplace and job. The job-specific training typically starts a day or two after the initial HR orientation.

3. *They effectively manage the expectations of new employees.* Two industrial psychologists, Kenneth N. Wexley of Michigan State University and Gary P. Latham, a Seattle-based consultant, found in their research that new employees, particularly those in first jobs, often have unrealistically high expectations about the amount of challenge and responsibility they will have on the job. Organizations, they suggest, must either make entry-level jobs more challenging or align new-hire expectations from the "get go." There is a good argument that this kind of realistic expectation setting should begin even before orientation, in the selection process. It should continue through their initial experiences with the supervisor once they start doing the job.

Wexley and Latham have data to support the wisdom of making anxiety reduction one of the goals of an orientation program. They report that in an experiment at Texas Instruments, several groups of new employees went through a special six-hour, question-and-answer, give-and-take, getting-to-know-the-company session in addition to a traditional corporate orientation program. The focus was placed on understanding the "real ropes" of the organization and what to expect from the boss and peers on the job the next day. A year later, they found that these employees had learned their jobs faster and had higher production and lower absence rates than did employees who had gone through a more traditional new-hire orientation.

The Adoption Metaphor

The hiring process may be all about survival of the fittest, but as you move from selection to orientation, it's important to leave the Darwinian mindset behind and begin thinking more in terms of *adoption,* or how you can best assimilate new hires into existing groups. Consider using the ADOPT acronym as a guide as you develop or tweak your orientation process for improved results:

Affirm the new employee for making the wise decision to be part of your organization or team.

Debrief the new employee for service insights. New employees enter your organization with "fresh eyes" that allow them to see things in your service delivery system that grizzled veterans might miss or discount as "part of the furniture." As the proverb says, *a guest sees more in an hour than the host in a year.* Asking for new hires' input also sends an early message that you value their opinions.

Orient your new hires to the values, standards, vision, and norms of the organization, not simply policies, procedures, and benefits. People want to know what the organization stands for and how they should tailor their behavior to best support that mission.

Partner the new employee with someone from outside his or her work group to show them the ropes beyond their unit and act as a "big brother or sister" for a few weeks.

Tribe. Borrowing from a Native American tradition that gave young braves a special task or challenge to mark their readiness to join the tribe, identify an assignment or project that a new hire can perform that has special meaning and makes a contribution to the team. It's critical that there is real work ready and waiting for people after the "Hi, how are ya? Glad you're gonna be with us!" stuff is over.

"Nothing is more frustrating to someone full of enthusiasm for a new job than sitting around stacking paper clips," say researchers Wexley and Latham.

There is an old shibboleth that states: "Well begun is half done." When it comes to getting a new employee off on the right foot and tracking with your organization's service focus, well begun is a lot more than half done. It may well be the most important first impression you can make.

> An employee is never more focused, malleable, and teachable than the first day on the job.
>
> —Horst Schulze
> CEO of Capella Hotels and
> Founder of Ritz-Carlton Hotels

18

Training Creates Competence, Confidence, and Commitment to Customers

Excellence is an art won by training and habituation. We are what we repeatedly do. Excellence, then, is not an act, but a habit.

—Aristotle

Nothing good happens for your customers or your organization until an employee makes it happen. Whether those employees are meeting face to face with customers or worrying over systems in the bowels of the organization, it is their skill and effort that make the difference between a Knock Your Socks Off Service organization and wishful thinking. Developing, honing, and keeping a competitive edge on your people's skills makes strategic sense.

It's not surprising, then, that in "service successful" organizations, training and development of employees are seen as a never-ending process that includes formal and on-the-job training, guided experience, effective coaching, targeted performance review, and strong support for learning from the organization. These companies know that if they're going to boast of superior service quality in their marketing or advertising campaigns, they better back it up with a staff trained to deliver the goods.

Providing better training and more of it for your people can and does create a big advantage in the marketplace. According to one study, employees who receive formal job training reach "standard" performance levels faster (72 percent faster), create less waste (70 percent less), and are better at customer troubleshooting and problem solving (130 percent better) than employees who learn their jobs through the tried and true—and very inefficient—"sit by Sally and ask questions" approach. In addition, there is pretty good evidence that employees who receive a significant amount of training on a regular basis—between twenty and forty hours a year—stay with you longer and receive higher marks in knowledge, skill, and hustle from customers.

Training in What?

Despite its importance as a competitive advantage, however, don't confuse training with mother love, chicken soup, or high-octane gasoline. It is not the case that if a little is good, a lot is better. Relevance counts as much as, maybe more than, minutes. To be effective, training should support serving customers better, working smarter, or creating better outcomes for the organization.

There are four kinds of skills your customer contact employees need to do their jobs well: technical skills, interpersonal skills, product and service knowledge, and customer knowledge. *All* are critical to their success. *All* need to be addressed throughout each individual's career with you. Following are some tips for developing and honing those four crucial skill areas.

Technical Skills

- *Technology.* Today's front liners need to be more technology savvy than ever before. For many service roles, that means mastering the latest software and the ability to deftly navigate the Web and communicate effectively with customers via instant chat, e-mail, text, and social media. It can also include knowing the ins and outs of hand-held technologies, copiers, scanners, cash registers (if you are a retailer), iPads, Blackberry devices, mobile apps, and telephone systems.

Implication: Assume nothing about your people's knowledge of your systems. Even if they've worked with a similar technology, they haven't yet worked with your particular variation on the system theme. What they don't know can kill you with customers.

- *Online Forms and Paperwork.* Employees need to understand the purpose of your records and systems—electronic and hardcopy—not just which blanks to fill in with what letters and numbers. They need to know what role customer histories, status, and incident reports; data integrity and privacy considerations; and forms filled out by or for the customer play in your system of information management. Any time that forms can affect the speed, reliability, and personal attention provided to customers, your people definitely need to know your forms and procedures cold.

Interpersonal Skills

- *People Skills.* We're hoping you hired your service people for their abilities to listen, understand, communicate, and relate with customers as well as their technical and product skills. No matter how good their specific skills may be, the more training, the more knowledge, and the more experience you can give your frontline people, the stronger their skills will become, particularly in dealing with the most complex or emotionally charged service situations.

The burden need not fall on you alone. A wide variety of books, simulation-based e-learning programs, DVDs, audio CDs, and low-cost seminars exists to remediate poor skills and polish competent ones toward mastery.

Caution: Training sometimes is met with resistance, especially when it is perceived as an attempt to "fix" problems people don't know or admit they have. Even experienced employees need their people skills brushed up from time to time—such training should be seen as natural and supportive, not a reaction to a deficiency.

• *Self-Assessments.* Give your people a mirror in which to view their current performance levels. Encourage employees who deal with customers over the phone to record several conversations and evaluate them alone or with the help of an experienced peer. Use videotaped role plays to let them see themselves as others see them. Pass along customer comments, the results of mystery shops, and your own analysis and observations in a direct, timely, and positive manner.

• *Teamwork.* With a little training in the proper way to give another person feedback, coworkers can help each other brush up on person-to-person skills. *Do not,* however, make this a requirement. People are generally apprehensive about receiving a job skills critique, especially when there is a possibility that the news will be less than thrilling. It is a tough spot to put a peer or pal in. The secret is to separate performance from person. Focusing on the former builds up skills. Concentrating on the latter tears down self-esteem.

• *Self-Directed Learning.* Give experienced employees the time and space (a couple of hours a month and a conference room will do) to role play different customer situations with each other, share tips and tricks, and generally talk shop. Don't attend these meetings yourself. The goal is for your people to learn from and with each other. That can't happen in the presence of the boss, no matter how "unthreatening" you think you are.

At Cabela's, the seller of outdoor recreation items that has become a phenomenon in states where it opens new stores, much of the knowledge accumulated by the crack floor sales staff is developed through peer-based training. Cabela's sales-people are encouraged to borrow products for a month—be it a tent, a canoe, or a fly fishing rod—and ask the same questions a customer might pose in order to learn more about the items. After the field test is over, employees fill out forms detailing the products' "highs and lows" and then give a presentation to coworkers about what they've learned. The feedback is also entered into "item notes," Cabela's knowledge management system that both in-store and call center employees can tap into to answer customer questions faster and more effectively.[41]

Product and Service Knowledge

• *Technical Aspects.* Customers expect your employees to know more about the products and services you sell than they do. That's not always the case, however, which is one of the prime reasons so many people prefer shopping by website or catalog to shopping in stores these days.

• *Competitive Aspects.* Customers also expect your front liners to know something about the products and services your competitors sell. The more knowledge and factual information (as opposed to sales hype and "fluff and nonsense") they can give your customers, the less need your customers will feel for comparison shopping.

• *Customer Buy Points.* Do your employees know what questions customers most frequently ask about your products and services? And how to answer them? Do they have a list or file of common complaints about your offerings and your competitors' products? Training can help them better anticipate and address customer needs or expectations.

Customer Knowledge

• *Customer profiles.* Your customer contact people in particular can never know too much about their customers, whether that involves the personal tastes of a consumer or the products and services of a business-to-business client. Your front liners should be trained to develop a "style" for asking questions about customers and to write down what they learn. Customers expect your people to "stay told."

- *Heavy Hitters.* Encourage customer contact people to create files on each of their five best customers, with notes on what they've learned about them. What common elements do they notice that are missing from other customers? Would nurturing those traits build business as well as customer loyalty?

Where Training Comes From

Knowing your people should be trained and getting them trained are separate issues.

- If your organization has a training department that delivers the type of training your employees need, that's a big plus. But that doesn't mean you're free to give the responsibility to someone else and wash your hands of involvement. You are responsible for ensuring that the right skills are taught and that they are applied correctly on the job. (For information on how you accomplish all that, stay tuned for the next chapter.)
- If you are in a small company, or one with no formal employee training department or system, you are de facto the training director, administrator, instructor, and facilitator, all rolled into one. You can, of course, pass some of the tasks to a senior or lead employee. But it's not a "short straw" situation— training is too important to be done poorly or by people who don't want the responsibility. You and/or your trainer designate will need to learn how to do effective job instruction training, called "train the trainer" training. Local universities, community or junior colleges, and vocational/technical schools can provide you with such training or refer you to an institution that does.

Successful Knock Your Socks Off Service companies are not only great performers, but learning companies as well.

Their people are encouraged to be knowledge sponges, sopping up new information at every turn. They know you never know where you'll find an edge, so they look everywhere and all the time. You should, too.

> The expense of training isn't what it costs to train employees. It's what it costs not to train them.
>
> —Philip Wilber
> retired President of Drug Emporium, Inc.

19

Thinking and Acting Like a Coach

Coaching subordinates isn't an addition to a manager's job; it's an integral part of it.

—George S. Odiorne

The definition of "boss" begins to take shape in most of us long before we get to the job market. It starts with "father" and "mother," then progresses to "teacher," "principal," and "coach." It may eventually include "professor," "scoutmaster," or "drill instructor." By the time we get to the work world, most of what we know about "bossing" has been shaped by people on whom we were dependent and times when someone else had close to complete control over our immediate actions and longer term destiny. Small wonder that "boss" for most employees is a four-letter word!

From Boss to Leader

Directing the performance of a service, rather than supervising the production of a product, calls for a different management orientation. "Leading" a service performance isn't directly leading in the sense of being that someone out front, with everybody else falling into line behind you. Rather, service management requires leadership skills more often associated with indirect management—coaching a team, teaching a skill, conducting an orchestra, or directing a play. In high-performing service organizations, managers need essentially the same skills that coaches use to bring out the best in a performing artist or athlete.

Clipboards and Whistles

The similarities between service managers in business and coaches in athletics and the arts are many—and worth exploring as you try to give yourself a frame of reference for your managerial actions and responsibilities. Like a coach:

- *You instill fundamentals.* Your people have to know how to play their particular roles or positions: what to do, and when, and how, what to say, and why. They need to know where to be when the customer feeds them a cue or throws them a curve. And just as great actors and athletes know the necessity of constant practice, of "getting in the reps" that help them master the part they are called on to play, you have to keep your people focused on the task and constantly honing their skills.

- *You build teamwork.* The second baseman is one of nine players on the baseball field. The violinist sitting first chair is just one player in the orchestra. No matter how individually talented he or she may be, the overall success of the production, be it the playing of a baseball game or a Beethoven symphony, is judged by how well everyone plays together. You position your players. You have to make sure they know how their role interlocks with others on the service team. You have to keep them focused on both their individual performance and the overall success of the group; keep the group working together in harmony in competitive conditions that challenge each employee in different ways.

- *You evaluate and adjust.* Every team, every individual performer, starts with a "game plan." But, typically, the plan can only prepare; it can't control play from start to finish. There are other variables, often outside anyone's control, that have to be taken into account in the midst of the performance. Like a coach, a service manager has to know how and when to replace or reposition players, change the script, react to immediate needs, and anticipate circumstances that may be encountered in the next quarter or the next act.

• *You reinforce and motivate.* The coach's role is to plan and prepare, react and adjust, correct problems without destroying the player's self-confidence, and praise good efforts without giving the recipient of the "well done's" a swelled head. You can't play favorites and build a united team. You can't preach sacrifice and dedication and then go put your feet up while your people give everything they've got. Your words and actions set the tone for theirs.

• *You're on the sidelines.* When the manager walks onto the playing field in most sports, play promptly stops. It doesn't continue until the coach has returned to the dugout, or the bench, or the wings. Just as you can't direct the play from the balcony or run the game from the locker room, you have to position yourself as close as you can to the action so you can support your players without either getting in their way or being so far removed that you don't know what they need from you.

Preparing for Success

Before they take the field or the stage, players have to have a good idea of what they're going to be doing and how their individual performances will combine into a cohesive group effort.

• In sports, that preparation involves knowing specific actions to take in specific circumstances—with a player on first, the shortstop throws to second base on a ground ball to get the double play; when there's no one on, the play is at first base.

• In the arts, there's a script or sheet of music to learn, often augmented by marks to hit when delivering a line or modifications to tempo and volume that provide subtle changes to the look and sound of the performance.

Business organizations prepare themselves in similar ways. At Disneyland and Walt Disney World, the young men and women who make the rides and attractions "go" work from carefully planned and memorized scripts, complete with exceptions, situational variations, and approved modifications— ad libs, in other words. They know where they're supposed to be and what they're supposed to do, including how to take charge of a potentially negative situation and turn it into a positive for their guests. Disney's service deliverers practice as a performance art. And that theme runs through training and management at every level.

Matching Performance to Coaching Technique

Since the performance of your people is your paramount concern as a coach, your style and actions have to change to respond to specific needs. Here are some ways to flex your style for maximum impact in different coaching scenarios:

• *When Your People Perform Well.* The adage "different strokes for different folks" is as true on the shop floor or in the call center as it is on the playing fields. When performance is superior and the performers are appropriately challenged, good coaches search for outcomes (or rewards) valued by each individual and adjust their managerial style to the styles of their people. The key is to understand your best performers well enough to identify the specific rewards they value and the techniques that work best for them. In many cases, the incentives or perks that motivate them will be far different from what you assume.

• *When Your People Perform Unevenly.* Every coach is faced with performers whose plays range from great in some aspects or at certain times to only average—sometimes less than average—in other areas. The appropriate technique is to reward the great stuff and to encourage improvement in the "only average"—*but not at the same time.*

When up-and-down performers hear, "Lou, you're doing great on *this,* but you can do better on *that,*" they often miss the kudos because their minds immediately lock on the "do better" part. Sometimes, in fact, they can interpret your compliments as a not-so-subtle bribe to get improvement—" I really want you to buckle down here, so I'll throw you a pointless compliment over there to disarm your resistance"— in which case, you risk losing the power of the reward as well as the focus on improvement. Separate the "reward" part from the "encourage" part, and you help your people glow *and* grow.

• *When Your People Hit a Slump.* Not even the best performers can do their best all the time. Sometimes they hit a slump or a lull during which everything seems to go wrong. When that happens, remember the classic coach's axiom: "If I traded players every time they were off, I'd wind up without a team in a hurry."

Good coaches patiently communicate continuous faith in the performer, especially when the results have been off and pride, confidence, and self-esteem are at their shakiest. They focus on and reinforce "the fundamentals"—the good efforts that will eventually pay off: "That's the way to go, Ann. Keep that up and I'm sure your sales (or service ratings, or retention/problem resolution rates) will improve."

Much has been written about the power of the coach's expectations on performance. It seems clear that a *demonstrated* belief in people can help elevate their performance levels. If you think people will succeed—because you've put them in a position to do just that—and you treat them that way, you're generally not going to be disappointed. The reverse is equally true: Expect the worst and you'll have a very good chance of getting it.

• *When Your People Try and Fail (and **They** Don't Know Why).* This condition calls for the coach to function as a mentor. The Greek poet Homer tells us that Mentor was the trusted counselor of Odysseus (Ulysses), under whose disguise Athena became the guardian and teacher of Telemachus, his son and heir, while Odysseus sailed away to fight in the Trojan War. Mentor was known for his wisdom and sensitivity. Consequently, the word today is used to describe "a wise and trusted adviser." The challenge of the coach-as-mentor is to communicate wisdom and experience without creating defensiveness and resistance in the performer.

There are many aspects to mentoring. One key is to give counsel in a manner that allows it to be heard, minimizes defensiveness, and keeps accountability for improvement with the performer. A useful approach for achieving such a tall order is to *first* get the performer's permission to give advice and *then* provide the advice as an "I" statement ("If I were you, I would . . ."). That's less telling and judgmental than an authoritarian "you should, you ought to, you had better" posture. Most performers, especially those confident in their skills and accustomed to succeeding, resent being told what to do.

Managers sometimes bristle at the suggestion that they should solicit permission from their people before giving advice to them. Who works for whom here, they ask. (If you're seeing your employees as customers of your managerial actions, not subjects on a feudal fief, the answer to that question should be obvious.)

The rationale is twofold:

1. The performer may actually know what to do despite your perception that he or she does not. *Unneeded* advice becomes *unheeded* advice.

2. This way, the coach keeps control and accountability with the performer, avoiding the surly look that says, "If you're so dang smart, why don't *you* do it."

• *When Your People Try and Fail (and **You** Don't Know Why).* This condition calls for astute analysis before action. A careful assessment of the performer and the performance often reveals unsuspected gaps in some ingredient required for high performance. Many managers faced with performance problems react in knee-jerk fashion by ordering up more training for the troops, but skill or knowledge deficiencies are only one among a litany of potential causes for service breakdown on the front lines. Here are eight variables to consider in searching for gaps between the performance required and the performance being delivered.

1. *Role–Person Mismatch.* Reexamine whether the performer would be more successful in a different role or on a different team.

2. *Task Clarity.* Perhaps the performer is not clear on the performance you require. Would you bet your next year's salary that *your* view of their accountabilities and expectations matches *their* view of those key parameters?

3. *Task Priority.* Sometimes failure is due to the performer's perception that the performance you expect is not really of high importance. Does their view of what's important match yours?

4. *Competence.* Failure can sometimes be due to a skill deficiency. People can't do well if they don't know how. The late training guru Robert Mager offers an easy test to determine whether you're facing a skill problem or a motivation issue: "Could they do the job if their life depended on it? If no, you have a performance problem. If yes, you may have a performance gap no amount of training can correct."

5. *Commitment.* Failure can indeed reflect a will deficiency. Low desire or a lack of motivation can erode performance to the point that you get compliance, but little commitment. Have you given performers a sense of ownership and control over the work they do? Do they know "why" what you expect is expected (the rationale of the task)?

6. *Obstacles.* Real or imagined barriers can interfere with good performance. To the extent that you, as the coach, can modify or remove them, you can free your people to perform better. If you empower *them* to remove barriers, you build an even greater sense of ownership and responsibility among your front liners.

7. *Reward for Failure.* Sometimes there's more reward for poor performance than good performance. People who get attention (however negative) when they do poorly and are ignored when they do well may stop doing well just to get a reaction. (If you've ever seen a "worst performer" award become more cherished than the "best performer" award, you've seen the dynamic in action.) You need to catch people doing well, too.

8. *Performance Feedback.* Do you provide clear, rapid information that helps your people evaluate and fine-tune their performance? Is it useful and presented from a consistent perspective? Or pointlessly general and subject to weather vane swings in emphasis that can confuse and disorient your staff?

If analysis fails to produce a reasonable explanation for substandard performance and does not suggest a path to a solution, a sit-down counseling session—focusing on the performance in question, not the personality or psychology of the person involved—should be the next step.

• *When Your People Don't Try (or Try to Fail).* The last condition of performance analysis is the most complex and carries a tone of "acting like a psychologist," so tread lightly here.

This condition could be rooted in performer hostility—toward the coach, toward the team, toward the customer, or even inward, toward self.

It might be due to burnout—cumulative stress and the absence of emotional support.

Sometimes it occurs when people view the performance standards set for them as arbitrary or capricious or believe that as soon as they settle in to one performance level, the standard will be raised again, systematically outpacing their capacity to keep measuring up.

If none of these scenarios is the case, and you have tried all the appropriate actions without success, only then should you resort to official reprimands to attempt to pull performance back up to acceptable levels.

Reprimands are designed to stop negative performance, but in such a way that performance can be improved *without* undermining self-esteem or leaving scar tissue. As Ken Blanchard, author of the *One Minute Manager* series of books, is fond of saying, reprimanded performers should respond by focusing on what they need to do to improve, not on how they were treated by the person delivering the bad news.

Most good books on discipline tell us that reprimands:

- Should be delivered in private.
- Should focus on performance rather than the person.
- Should be given with frankness, but not in anger.
- Should be appropriate to the infraction.

Good coaches do all of that and one more thing: They underscore the impact an individual's poor performance has on the team's performance. They know that it is far better to have people working hard to avoid letting down their teammates— or to meet their own high standards of performance—than to make them sweat to impress their coach.

The game of human achievement is played with complex players, changing rules, and ambiguous measurements. The coaches we admire on the sidelines at Sunday's game or behind the performance of a talented artist or performer have much to teach us that is relevant for Monday's corporate game.

> I spend most of my time thinking about what will motivate players.
>
> —Pat Riley
> Head Coach, Miami Heat, 1995–2003
> and 2005–2008

Imperative 6

Involve, Empower, and Inspire

Involvement is the enfolding of an employee in the decisions as well as the work of the organization. Think about it. If two heads are better than one, what could happen if *everyone* who works for you focused their brain power on your biggest problem?

Involved employees willingly think beyond the rudimentary features of their jobs and take on the role of problem finder and solver. But involvement is a two-way tunnel. Employees who are encouraged to be part of a problem-finding, problem-solving, or new idea effort expect to have their ideas taken seriously. Any hint that an involvement effort is employee relations window dressing quickly kills commitment.

Empowerment is working *with* your people to enable them to perform beyond simple rules—to act intelligently, not out of habit, routine, or fear. Empowerment is neither a gift nor unlimited

license. It is an act of development, a matter of helping employees feel an increased sense of control over their work, decisions,
and environment in general.

"I'm sorry sir, I just follow orders" is the stock answer of an
employee in a "don't think, just follow the rules" organization.
"Let me see what I can do about that" is the signature of
empowered employees working on behalf of *their* customers.

Inspiration is the process of creating excitement, enthusiasm,
and commitment to the customer and customer service.
Inspiration does not require a manager or leader with a charismatic style or magnetic personality. However, it does take a
manager who demonstrates through word and deed that great
customer service is an obvious priority. To paraphrase humorist
Will Rogers, "People learn from observation not from conversation." Employees do not watch your mouth, they watch your
moves. Make your moves in sync with a reverence for customers
and a zeal to serve them well.

20

Fostering Responsible Freedom

Sooner or later you have to trust your people.
—Jim Barksdale
CEO of Barksdale
Management Corporation

Bill had worked through lunch so he could get back to his hotel to change clothes for an important dinner meeting in a nearby town. He was staying on one of those fancy upper floors, the concierge level as they liked to call it. By 4:30 P.M., he'd made the quick change and realized he had almost half an hour before the client was to pick him up. Having skipped lunch and with dinner still several hours away, he realized he was starving! Not to worry, he figured. The concierge floor had a lounge area that provided small sandwiches and spicy meatballs to guests. A quick snack and a soda would tide him over.

Alas, Bill had not figured on the prickliness of the guardian of the concierge lounge. "Hors d'oeuvres," she informed him with all the pointless authority of the petty bureaucrat she apparently aspired to be, "are served from 5 P.M. We're not ready to open yet."

Over the rumblings of an empty stomach, Bill started to explain his plight. "It's wonderful that the hotel is willing to

163

lay out such a nifty spread," he said. Yes, he certainly understood the rules, he acknowledged. "But since the chafing
dishes are obviously already hot and full, and the plates and
silver ready and waiting, we could surely jump the gun by a
few minutes, right?"

"Sorry," came the reply in a tone of voice that made it
clear she wasn't. "I don't make the rules. You'll just have to
miss out, I guess." And with that, three very bright, positive
days in that hotel turned ugly brown, done in by an employee
more concerned with policies and procedures than serving
and satisfying customers. Bill hasn't been back to that hotel
since, nor will he be stopping by anytime soon. He's taking his
business someplace else these days.

Was the woman genuinely nasty, mean, and awful? Or
was she just another unempowered employee, afraid all heck
would break loose if she sidestepped policy and passed out a
single meatball twenty minutes before the posted time? It's
hard to know from the here and now. But we do know that
genuinely empowered frontline employees are the ones who
most genuinely delight in shaving this corner and bending
that minor rule to make a customer happy. And the managers
of genuinely empowered people are the ones most prone to
aid and abet them at every turn.

What Empowerment Is—and Is Not

Many managers have an ongoing and often irrational fear of
the "E" word—*empowerment*. They have heard one too many
speaker and seen one too many film suggesting that "empowered employees" are simply inmates placed in charge of the
asylum, set forth unbounded by rules to "do whatever it takes
to make the customer happy."

What are they afraid of? The predictable things, of course:
that employees who are turned loose will give the store away to
conniving customers or that they'll try to buy customer satisfaction at the expense of profit, ducking the hard and nasty work of
telling a customer no when that's the right (or only) answer.

Our experience (and we've yet to encounter anyone
whose own experience doesn't agree) has been that customer

service people seldom do such things—*if* they are well trained and managed and if empowering them is a process rather than a pronouncement.

Empowerment is the self-generated exercising of professional judgment and discretion on the customer's behalf. It is doing what needs to be done rather than simply doing what one has been told to routinely do. From the manager's perspective, empowerment is a key element in the process of releasing the expression of personal power at the front lines. It is the opposite of enslavement.

Because personal power is already present within the individual, empowerment is not a gift one gives to another. To the contrary, personal power is released when managers and supervisors remove the barriers that prevent its expression. The distinction is important because it focuses us more on what we take away from the system than what we give to our people (Figure 20-1).

What does empowerment look like? An empowered act, by definition, is exercising initiative beyond or outside the conventional norm. Confidently following the policy may be appropriate, and quite frequently satisfying, to a customer seeking nothing more than the standard offering. But it is not an empowered act.

Empowerment kicks in when the customer's long-term loyalty is at risk because of an unforeseen problem or unanticipated request. It's also at work in the little value-addeds that can make

Empowerment Is NOT a Gift		
• Something You Encourage	NOT	• Something You Give
• Congruence	NOT	• Compliance
• Consistency	NOT	• Conformance
• Accepted	NOT	• Assigned
• Partnership	NOT	• Parental
• Values Oriented	NOT	• Rules Oriented
• Right Things	NOT	• Easy Things
• Appropriately	NOT	• Correctly

Figure 20-1. Empowerment Is Not a Gift.

the most ordinary of service transactions extraordinarily memorable and positive for the customer.

E Is for Excellence

Service quality research over the past two decades has shown empowerment to have many benefits:

- An empowered employee can more effectively manage the customer relationship and turn superficial contact into a true partnership than one who must constantly balance instincts to "do the right thing" against the fine print of a policy and procedure manual.

- To the customer, an empowered employee is a powerful commentary on the whole service orientation of the organization. Nothing sets an upset customer's blood boiling faster—particularly one who's already invested significant time and energy trying to solve a problem or get an answer—than hearing a frontline employee say, "I'll have to check with my manager." Empowered people send a message that a business truly does put customers first. Unempowered people tell customers that the organization has so little regard for its customer contact staff that managers are unwilling to give them the power to make customers happy.

- To the employee, empowerment has significant effects on self-esteem and morale and carries a strong message about management's priorities and behavioral style. As the University of Maryland's Benjamin Schneider has repeatedly demonstrated: *Treat your people like gold—or dirt—and they'll treat the customer accordingly.*

Today, more than ever before, we want and need people whose sense of responsibility to serve the customer takes precedence over a jumble of organizational red tape. It's up to managers to strip away the layers of organizational inertia that have calcified over the years so people can do that in a professional way that benefits themselves, their customers, and the organization.

Letting It Happen

"How do I empower my employees?" is a question as flawed as "How do I motivate my employees?" It may be even *more* flawed, since eliminating "boss control" is at the core of empowerment and the "how do I" part of the question, no matter how well intended, still reeks of "boss control." So where and how does real empowerment start? And what can a manager do to see that it starts at all? A short story will help explain the forces at work.

A patient at Aurora St. Luke's Medical Center in Milwaukee lost an inexpensive but favorite pair of sneakers during his stay. Housekeeping, after learning of the man's complaint, concluded that someone had mistakenly thrown out the sneakers and was quick to offer a heartfelt apology. Not good enough. Offers to pay for the patient's sneakers also were not satisfactory. The patient wanted *those* sneakers.

At that point, the traditional response would likely have been a diplomatically insipid form letter saying something along the lines of "Thank you for bringing this matter to our attention. Your satisfaction is our only goal. If we can ever . . ." and making it clear that reasonable people had done all that could reasonably be expected over a pair of sneakers. End of story.

Instead, a young part-time housekeeper who had been involved in some of the phone calls over the incident took over. Acting on his own and not on a managerial directive, he got a detailed description of the sneakers from the patient, left work, went to a store, and, using his own money, purchased a replacement pair of identical shoes.

The patient was surprised. And elated. And the young part-time housekeeper? He received St. Luke's first ever award for the most meritorious act of empowered behavior. It's called the Golden Sneaker Award.

That's what empowerment looks like. No one "gave" permission for the housekeeper to leave work to go buy sneakers. He exercised the personal power he had always had on the customer's behalf. He thought first and foremost about what was really at issue—a pair of shoes, not assessing internal blame or hewing to the strict interpretation of hospital policy over patient claims of lost items.

By choosing to celebrate his action on an organizational scale, managers at St. Luke's sent the message that this kind of behavior is not aberrant or suspect. It's an example of what everyone can and should do if the hospital is to continue to attract patients.

Of course, not all your employees will be as eager as the St. Luke's housekeeper to go above and beyond to satisfy customers. As much as they might dream of taking such bold actions, the reality is that when push comes to shove, many of your people would rather someone simply tell them what to do rather than devising creative solutions themselves. Others might resist because of "doing more with less" work environments—they feel like their work plates are already overflowing and replicating the housekeeper's actions doesn't feel plausible given the strict productivity and efficiency goals they're expected to meet.

So how can you get more frontline employees to take the initiative with customers? One way is to treat them more like partners than subordinates. Position-based power management—the "because I said so" type—is fast becoming the last resort of the inept. One of the quickest ways for employees to learn whether they are really empowered or not is to make a visible mistake in the name of pleasing customers. If the error is met with rebuke and punishment—if the empowered decision is denigrated by a superior—it sends quite a different message than if the manager sees it as an opportunity for learning or improved problem solving.

That doesn't mean you should give employees unlimited license to please customers—some elastic guidelines are still required. The manager who says "just do what you think is best" is more likely demonstrating abdication (or fatigue at the end of a long work day) than empowerment. The goal should be to give your people "responsible freedom" defined by clear, real-world examples of how they might fix customer problems in a variety of service situations—without first coming to the boss for the green light.

Today's new partner leaders focus less on sovereignty and more on support, with controlling behaviors taking a back seat to a coaching mindset. If empowering people truly is your goal, it's a leadership model you would do well to emulate.

> Our people in the plants are responsible for their own output and its quality. We expect them to act like owners.
>
> —Ken Iverson
> author, *Plain Talk: Lessons from a Business Maverick*

21

Removing the Barriers to Empowerment

Never tell people how to do things. Tell them what to
do and they will surprise you with their ingenuity.

—General George Patton, Jr.

A customer walked into a crowded fast-food restaurant and ordered a sandwich, small fries, and soft drink to go. Told there would be a short wait, he stepped aside while the counter clerk waited on others. By the time half a dozen customers had worked their way past him, he was losing patience. Fast food, eh?

Finally, his slow burn now beginning to fog nearby windows, his takeout order was ready. As he stepped to the counter, prepared to provide a little direct feedback on his service experience, he was met with his bag, a confident smile, and a surprise: "I'm very sorry you had to wait," said the high school student who had taken his order. "I know you're in a hurry. Because you had to wait, I gave you a large order of fries instead of a small one. I hope you'll come back real soon."

Anger? Gone. Impression? Positive. What kind of place is this, where seventeen-year-olds can diagnose and disarm upset customers on the spot, on their own—and apparently with no need to protect the return on the restaurant's potato investment?

It's a Hardee's, actually. One of thousands where they teach people, "Don't fight, make it right." The extra fries didn't disappear into the inventory ozone. They were accounted for—on a pad of "Saved Customer" forms. Built into the Hardee's approach to fast food is a recognition that customers have plenty of alternatives these days and a conscious decision that an extra helping of fries, a larger soft drink, or an occasional cookie on the house is a relatively inexpensive but very effective way to make sure they come back again when things don't quite turn out right.

Notice that the responsibility for turning that corporate mindset into action rests squarely on the shoulders of the seventeen-year-olds (and thirty-four-year-olds, and sixty-three-year-olds) who work the counters and the drive-throughs, typically at or near minimum wage pay scales, and without benefit of a couple of years in an MBA program. How does Hardee's give that sense of empowerment to those kinds of frontline workers?

It doesn't. The power is already there with the people who tally the orders and bag the food and fill the soft drink cups. What Hardee's has done is remove the barriers that prevent frontline service professionals from taking action when their own observations of what their customer is experiencing tell them that action is indicated.

If *your* employees come to work with adequate power to act with responsible freedom, what prevents this power from being used? Something obviously gets in the way. The key to the manager's role *vis-à-vis* empowerment is found in understanding the barriers and then working to remove them.

The task at hand is to encourage the directed use of responsible freedom on the customer's behalf. The challenge is one of coordination: getting employees to act with responsible freedom *and* in ways that benefit the customer plus the organization. It's not an impossible quest. Here are four consistent reasons that frontline employees fail to act in empowered ways—four "P" words that sum up the ways organizations have in the past effectively said no to their people's empowered instincts: no purpose, no protection, no permission, and no proficiency.

No Purpose

People will act with power if they experience a greater purpose in their work than simply the day-to-day task. For frontline employees to act with extraordinary zeal, they must believe that it is their purpose to "make a customer happy" or to "make the service or product work like it's supposed to." Purpose is the "Oh, so *that's* why I'm here" explanation that energizes and motivates.

FedEx founder and chairman Fred Smith tells his employees, "We transport the most important cargo in the world—an organ for a vital transplant, a gift for a special ceremony, a factory part that may have halted a major enterprise." Employees take that service vision seriously, as evidenced by the actions of FedEx courier Joe Kinder during a raging snowstorm. The storm had shut down the city, but Kinder had an important delivery—visas for a couple traveling to Russia to adopt their son. The weather prevented the package from arriving on the expected day, and the couple was due to leave for Russia the next morning. The situation was dire; without the visas, the couple couldn't adopt the child.

With things looking bleak and the service promise echoing in Kinder's mind—"precious packages have to be delivered on time"—he decided to take action. After some investigative work, Kinder tracked the package down and, despite dangerous road conditions, drove out to the couple's home and delivered the visas to an ecstatic response. His actions allowed the couple to leave on time and bring home their new son.

Here's how you can instill a sense of purpose in your own work group:

1. Talk about your vision often. Focus on what you want the organization to *be*, not just what you want it to *do*.
2. When communicating expectations, describe the "whys" as well as the "whats" and "whens."
3. Recognize corporate heroes by "telling their stories"—the details of their special accomplishments that become examples for others to follow.

4. Live the mission by making sure your daily actions are consistent with the purpose you've set for your people. Examine how you spend your time, what you show excitement about, and what you worry about. Your actions telegraph your true priorities to those around you.

No Protection

Jerry Harvey, an iconoclastic professor at George Washington University, maintains that resistance to change is a myth. "It is not change people resist; it is the prediction of pain," says Harvey. A consistent barrier to employees acting with power is their prediction of pain: "If I make the wrong decision, no safety net will catch me."

As a manager, you need to reduce the risk factor your employees may associate with empowered actions. Even if it makes you tense up and cross your fingers to think of them out there on the high wire, your job is to reinforce their courage and commitment so they go out and try again.

What you can do:

1. Examine your procedures. Employees may feel unprotected due to past practice. Punish an infraction, and if you are not careful, you will create a precedent. Are employees clear on the difference between what is a "thou shalt not . . ." and what is an "it would be better if you didn't . . ."?
2. Recall the last few times an employee made an honest mistake. Was the error met with reproach and guilt, or was the mistake treated as an opportunity for learning and growth? Is forgiveness for mistakes directly spoken or just tacitly implied?
3. Are employees publicly given the benefit of the doubt? If your people were interviewed by an outsider, would they say they received more coaching or more critiquing? How many times do employees get praised for gallant efforts that failed to pan out as planned?

4. Are employees commended for seeking assistance from others, including those in superior positions? Managers should be a helpful resource on call as needed, not a troll lurking under an organizational bridge that people fear disturbing for the havoc it might reek upon them.

No Permission

As a manager, you need to continually and explicitly give your people permission to act on the customer's behalf. It's dangerous to assume that employees will just know what they are and aren't allowed to do—or even that they'll believe you the first time you say, "Yes, you can." Employees have been hearing managers say no for generations through their experiences as customers as well as their on-the-job encounters. Empowerment takes some getting used to.

Organizations that turn front liners loose to solve customer problems, as well as regularly solicit front liners' ideas for boosting service quality, often reap impressive benefits. Some of the best notions for improving service come not from the strategists sitting on mahogany row, but from those who spend most of their days listening to customer problems and concerns. Tapping into their collective experience makes good business sense; most of your service reps will speak to more customers in one day than executives will in a year.

While the tendency is to think these suggestions will run toward the cost prohibitive or pie in the sky, our research shows that when front liners are asked for improvement ideas, most are as careful to consider costs of implementation as they are impact on customer satisfaction. And by regularly involving them in this way, you create a stronger sense of ownership and send a message that their experiences and opinions are valued—two factors research has shown to boost morale and retention rates.

At USAA, management regularly encourages customer service representatives to suggest changes that will improve the customer experience. One rep's recent idea to offer insurance premium billing that's timed to the military's biweekly paychecks (the insurer's core customer base) is just one of the many frontline suggestions the company has implemented over the years.[42]

What you can do:

1. Take to heart a line on the menu at McGuffey's Restaurant in Asheville, North Carolina: "The answer is yes, what's the question?" Apply that kind of thinking with your people. Model responsible freedom and measured risk taking through your actions. Where you lead by example, others will follow.
2. Examine your reward and recognition practices. Which is more valued: creativity or compliance? Being adroit and resourceful or being accurate and right? Who gets praised or promoted—and for what?
3. Use "zero-based" rule budgeting. If you eliminated all the rules, regulations, and policies attached to your employees' roles and then added back only those that are absolutely relevant, would you be writing restrictions long into the night?

No Proficiency

"Knowledge is power," said English poet Francis Bacon. The capacity to find clever, resourceful, and creative solutions is the mark of a wise person prepared and empowered to go beyond the traditional, the familiar, and the ordinary. Training your people, not once but constantly, provides not just competence but wisdom. And whereas competence promotes confidence, wisdom fosters power.

Author Malcolm Knowles tells the story of a medium-size manufacturer of radios and televisions that realized the electronics industry was on the eve of a sizable transition from vacuum tube to transistor technology. The company began to train heavily—even in courses that would not be approved according to most tuition refund policies. When the industry began to change over to transistors, this company quickly grabbed the dominant market share in the electronic appliance world. The company is Sony.

One reason that Sony's top brass gave for the company's meteoric rise was learning. They reasoned that the more people learned, the better learners they would become and the more likely they would want to learn. Sure enough, Sony employees learned new transistor skills at a much faster pace than their competitors. In addition, the more they learned, the more empowered employees felt. They had the courage needed to risk exploring new techniques and alternative approaches.

What you can do:

1. Emphasize proficiency, both by recognizing and rewarding those in your work group whose performance stands out and by using them as mentors and team leaders.
2. Be a lifelong learner yourself. Again, the example you set is the one your people will follow.
3. Develop a folklore of empowerment stories—anecdotal evidence that communicates (1) that empowered actions should be taken and (2) specific examples of how it may be done.

Our employees probably make more decisions in the hallways than most companies make behind closed doors.

—John Oren
Managing Partner,
Pinch Holdings

22

Inspiring Passion for the Customer

I'd rather have one person with passion than forty who are merely interested.

—E. M. Forster

Picture this: You walk out of the airport to take a taxi cab to the hotel. The taxi driver has a sullen look, seems completely disinterested in you, plays music you dislike, and talks to his buddies on his phone all the way. When you arrive at the hotel and ask for a receipt, he acts like he's doing you a big favor and then frowns at the tip!

Now substitute the taxi driver for any one of your employees. Do you have employees who seem to hate work, drag through the day like they are barely alive, show the enthusiasm of a tree stump, talk to their buddies while ignoring customers, and then get irritated when there is no raise?

Mediocrity can usurp the energy from passion and the opportunity from initiative. Leaders who tolerate mediocrity signal that their real standards are much lower than what they generally state. Organizations can in fact be populated by only winners. The proverbial bell-shaped curve of performance— that there will always be a small percentage of superstars and an equal number who do just enough to get by—is neither an organizational necessity nor a statistical requirement.

The leadership antidote to passion-free mediocrity may not be to change employees or telegraph your displeasure or even "crack the whip." Your employees may simply need to be inspired. And, one of the key roles of a leader is to provide inspiration—to be a fire starter, igniting passion and commitment.

Let's revisit the taxi driver. We have discovered that passengers can inspire drivers to give consistently great customer service. It works like this. The first step is your own **animation**—choosing to demonstrate the attitude you seek from the driver. Next, as you board the taxi, sincerely express you're **appreciation** ("Thank you for being my driver."). Tell the driver your destination and ask if he knows the location. When he says he does, deliver **affirmation** ("Terrific, I am dealing with a true professional."). The final part is a bit delicate. **Validation** is helping the driver view his role in a larger light than just driving a taxi. Keep it upbeat and optimistic. ("You have probably helped a lot of people as a driver, haven't you?"). Upon arrival, extend your hand for a handshake and then ask for a receipt. You'll be amazed at how quickly passion can be ignited. Liberty Mutual came out with a new ad campaign a few years ago. In it, ordinary people making their way through the day encounter someone doing something nice for someone else. With that fresh reminder of how good it feels to make someone's day a little nicer by extending simple common courtesy, a chain reaction of good deeds followed.

Animation: Inspiring through Modeling

Animation is "the process of bringing to life." We watch cartoons and are awed by the skill of the artist who can transform stills into life-like characters. The late Chuck Jones, creator of such famous cartoon characters as Bugs Bunny, Daffy Duck, Wile E. Coyote, and Road Runner, wrote: "The secret to making a character come alive is not how you draw that particular character. It happens when everything in the frame moves with the character."

Great service leaders begin by choosing to *insert* employee inspiration instead of seething about its absence. Like the cartoonist, they do this by illustrating enthusiasm. They make "everything in the frame move with the employee"—including their own attitude. They strive to be the inspired role model they want employees to emulate. Davy Crockett was an inspirer at the siege of the Alamo in 1836. Colonel Jim Bowie wrote in a letter to Governor Henry Smith, "David Crockett has been *animating* the men to do their duty." Remember, it is impossible to light a fire with a wet match!

Appreciation: Inspiring with Gratitude

"Thank you" is a phrase we all enjoy hearing. Most people do not hear it enough. However, instead of just saying the words, take one more step. Let the person know exactly what he or she did that warranted your gratitude. When we were eating at a restaurant, our waiter had on a name tag plus an additional tag proclaiming him to be the "employee of the month." "Congratulations," one of us said. "What did you do to warrant such an honor?" The waiter stood quietly and then said flatly, "I guess it was my turn." He had no idea what he had done to be recognized, so he knew of no special action he was being encouraged to repeat.

A few years ago we were consulting with a successful company whose average nonsupervisory professional employees were twenty-seven-year-olds who earned about $100,000 a year! Most were highly driven, Ivy League, college-educated go-getters. Yet, an employee-attitude survey revealed they regarded themselves as underrewarded. At first we thought we were dealing with spoiled brats who had no idea how the real world worked. But we were wrong. "We know we are very well compensated," they told us. "We just do not feel valued and recognized for what we do!"

A word of caution: As important as it is to show appreciation and let employees know how much you value the work they are doing, be careful to avoid the "Thank you, but . . ." syndrome. Do not fall into the habit of mixing gratitude and coaching together. They are two totally different pieces of the management puzzle. Every time you thank an employee and then suggest ways of doing something different or better, you've taken away all the benefit of saying thank you in the first place and the employee only hears, "I guess I messed that up." Be certain your thank you is genuine and specific and is not used as a segue to correct behavior.

Affirmation: Inspiring with Confidence

"Treat a man as he is, and he will remain as he is. Treat a man as he could be, and he will become what he should be," wrote Ralph Waldo Emerson. One of the most powerful phenomena in human behavior is the self-fulfilling prophesy (also called the Pygmalion effect). Little is really known about why it works as it does. However, your belief in your employees, demonstrated in behavior and attitude, has a major impact on their behavior. If you believe a person is going to be a winner and you treat him or her that way, that person generally does not disappoint you. If you believe a person is going to be a loser and you treat him or her that way, that person generally does not disappoint you. It is important how you communicate expectations through your actions.

Even your tone of voice and emphasis on key words can impact what employees hear and therefore interpret. Think of the line: "I think Bill can do it." Read the line six times, each time verbally emphasizing a different word in the sentence, and notice how it alters the meaning. This does not mean you have to censor every word you utter. It simply illustrates how the power of tone can reflect an attitude.

Validation: Inspiring with Purpose

This is the trickiest part. Leaders can change the content by expanding the context. What this means is that moving from specific to general can help someone view their world in a more optimistic, hopeful light. This is a technique parents use to get a child out of a pessimistic view. It is the positive version of "Well, you *could* be starving in Africa." Susie comes home fussing that Johnny is teasing her. Her mother coaches her that Johnny doesn't realize how very special she really is. The intent is elevating the focus to a grander, more glorious view.

As a leader, you can play a similar role. You have a chance to be fire starter—to inspire someone to deliver their very best.

Judy and Jane were working together in New York City and checked into a midtown hotel one evening. However, their approaches to check-in were completely different. Judy warmly approached the desk clerk with a Steinway smile and a jovial disposition. She made complimentary small talk with the desk clerk, making certain to use the desk clerk's name, which she eyeballed on his uniform jacket. Jane took a more somber route with the desk clerk at the other end of the front desk counter. Without a greeting, she put her credit card on the counter, filled out the paperwork in silence, and departed with a room key.

The plan was for the two women to go to their respective rooms, drop their luggage, and then rendezvous in Judy's room to go out for dinner. But, when Jane entered Judy's room, she was stunned. Judy had a suite four times the size of Jane's typical hotel room, plus it had a great view of Central Park.

"How did you get this big suite?" Jane inquired of her colleague. Judy humbly responded, "I wanted more than a typical room. I knew the front desk clerk really wanted me to have it; I just needed to inspire him." But, the story did not end there. When the two women returned from dinner, Judy's message light was on. It was the front desk clerk who had called to make sure her suite was satisfactory. Jane's message light was not on!

Inside every employee is passion waiting to be ignited; excellence waiting to be unleashed. Strike your leadership match—animation, appreciation, affirmation, and validation—and be warmed by the results.

> You want pistols, hot-blooded people bent on making their mark. Not mild mannered, conforming types who will succumb to the awesome power of the existing culture.
>
> —Price Pritchett

Imperative 7

Recognize, Reward, Incent, and Celebrate

Creating Knock Your Socks Off Service is a human endeavor. It happens when a group of people willingly and enthusiastically work together to create something none could accomplish alone. Human nature is a key factor. Understand it and respect it and it will work for you. Disregard it, ignore it, downplay its impact, and it will work against you.

The people who work for and with you want to do a good job. They want to work for an organization and in a department that is successful. They need something back in return. They need to know how they are doing: whether they are succeeding or failing, whether they are average or exemplary, and what they can do to improve when improvement is needed.

They need to be recognized and rewarded for both their accomplishments and their efforts—sometimes individually and sometimes as a part of a group effort.

And they need to be enfolded in something beyond their own ability to achieve through celebration of the effort and achievements of the corporate "all of us together."

23

Recognition and Reward: Fueling the Fires of Service Success

Recognition drives the human engine.

—Leonard Berry
Texas A&M University

"Catch somebody doing something right today" is an admonition that succinctly captures years of managerial wisdom and a ton of behavioral science research. It has special meaning and import for the service management effort. If you want people in your organization to think and act in customer-oriented ways, seek out ways to catch them doing just that, and reward and recognize them for making the effort.

It is a reasonable and rational guideline, a precept hard to disagree with—and one more easily broken than kept. The biggest problem, of course, is that in the modern service workplace most managers seldom see more than a small sample of employee behavior and therefore have few opportunities to personally catch employees, particularly frontline employees, doing *anything*—good, bad, or indifferent. You have to be prepared to use what you see as well as find ways to see more.

Research shows that many service employees leave their jobs simply because they feel unappreciated in their work. That makes finding small ways to show your people you value what they do each day in the name of pleasing customers one of the best—and most cost-effective—methods for reducing attrition levels and boosting performance.

Effective recognition and reward oil the wheels of willing cooperation and dedication to the job.

• *Reward* typically connotes money: salary and bonuses, cash awards, financial incentives, and other tangible payoffs in lieu of cash (though often chosen and presented in terms of their cash value).

• *Recognition* is typically less tangible, given for taking a little extra time with a customer, for going a step beyond nominal expectations, for caring about what the customer needs and expects to be done, and for looking for ways to do it better, faster, and/or smarter.

From Practice to Program

Recognition and reward come in as many styles as there are recognizers and rewarders. Common approaches include:

• *High-Profile Formal.* Programs such as "Bravo Zulu" and "Golden Falcon" (FedEx), "Circle of Service Excellence" (U.S. Bank), "Customer Champs" (Manheim), and "Heritage Award" (Great Plains Software, a Microsoft subsidiary) come complete with detailed rules and objectives that everyone learns and set prizes, payoffs, and awards that everyone can strive for.

Caution: Make sure your recognition spotlight doesn't put employees on the spot. If someone doesn't feel comfortable standing up to take a bow, respect their wishes.

• *Low-Profile Formal.* Little rewards can be as effective as the big ones if they are used the right way. Nonmonetary awards possess the "trophy value" that cold hard cash doesn't; while few people dislike cash and it provides a quick rush of satisfaction, the money usually disappears quickly and employees are left with nothing to remember their accomplishment. Lapel-style pins, plaques, framed certificates, and embossed business cards that list service awards are tactics common to service leaders. Others award good suggestions for new or better ways to serve customers with free video rentals, tickets to sporting or cultural events, courtesy time off, gift certificates, or points redeemable for merchandise at the company store. In one retail bank, the employee who submits the month's best idea wins a circulating trophy—a three-foot-high light bulb.

The trick is to avoid one-size-fits-all reward plans. Give employees a choice of awards so they can choose something that fits their tastes. One person's sporting event nirvana, for example, might be another's snooze-inducing "night that wouldn't end."

• *Informal.* A simple "thank you for your effort" note or a verbal "well done" delivered in front of coworkers are great ways of recognizing people. Style counts every bit as much as substance. A handwritten note from the CEO saying nothing more elaborate than "I really appreciate the extra effort you expended making the senior officers conference a success" is often more powerful—and certainly more lasting—than cash on the barrelhead. It's the sincerity and acknowledgment that count most to the recipient. Ditto for similar notes that you send to your frontline staff. In this day of ubiquitous e-mail, a heartfelt "thanks" note penned by hand can make a big impression.

Avoiding Reward Pitfalls

You'll also want to ensure your reward and recognition efforts don't fall prey to the law of unintended consequences. Organizations and managers sometimes can do more harm than good in how they choose to design or implement recognition plans. Beware of these pitfalls:

• *Winner Takes All Plans.* Competition is healthy in the marketplace, but it can be demotivating in the workplace.

Abandon employee of the month or other winner-take-all service reward plans in favor of those that recognize more people for the small things they do every day to please customers or assist coworkers.

• *Perception of Favoritism.* When peers have some say in the voting process for formal rewards, people tend to see the process as more open, honest, and fair than if a manager unilaterally chooses award recipients. After all, who better to identify the service stars (and slackers) than those working alongside them on the front lines?

• *Lack of Immediacy.* Waiting for weeks or months after someone exhibits commendable behavior to reward it dulls the impact. Deliver rewards or recognition as close to the contribution or event as possible.

• *Same Old, Same Old.* Even the most inventive and unique awards grow stale and lose their impact over time. Survey your employees to make sure they still see your reward or recognition plans as appropriately motivating. If the answer is no, develop other options to breathe new life into the program.

Lasting Value

Sometimes recognition and reward programs take on dimensions that show you just how valued they can be to employees. We once worked with a theme park that was researching various ways to put feedback and recognition into the workaday life of employees—and to improve customer satisfaction in the process. On the reward and recognize side, we started giving supervisors little cards called "Warm Fuzzies" to give to employees—you guessed it—caught "doing something good." Token givers were encouraged to write notes on the backs of the cards explaining what the receiver had done to merit a Warm Fuzzie. Four years later, we had supervisors giving out Warm Fuzzies, guests giving out Warm Fuzzies, and frontline employees giving Warm Fuzzies to each other as well as to supervisors and staff support people.

We encountered only one problem with the system. Hoarding. Not by the givers. By the recipients. Those "Warm Fuzzie" cards had point values and accumulated points could be redeemed for gifts and merchandise. But employees were not turning in the "Fuzzies" for the prizes. An employee focus group told us why. The psychological value of receiving the little cards outweighed the value of the prizes to many of the employees. As one employee put it, "When I'm having a bad day, I take out my stack of Warm Fuzzies and reread the notes on the backs, the nice things people said about me, and I feel better. That's more important than any prize I could buy for turning the cards in."

The solution was easy: give the employees credit for the points and let them keep the cards. It made a mess of our research, but it worked. The lesson was a big one: It's terribly easy to lose sight of how powerful a sincere "You did a good job—thanks" can be.

> The deepest principle of human nature is a craving to be appreciated.
>
> —William James

24

Feedback: Breakfast, Lunch, and Dinner of Champions

Hey! How'm I doin'?

> —Ed Koch
> former Mayor of New York City

We all need former Mayor Koch's question answered from time to time, especially about our workaday activities. We all like to know what bosses and peers think of our performance so we have some inkling if we're on the right—or wrong— track. As a manager, your people look to you for the information they need to (1) recognize and keep doing what they do well, (2) understand and improve what they do less well, and (3) stop doing the things that contribute little to unit or organizational goals.

Information that genuinely answers those "How am I doing?" questions—that your people can use to either *confirm* (call attention to good work) or *correct* (call attention to work that needs improvement) their performance—is called feedback. It comes in many forms and from a variety of sources:

- Some feedback is easy to get and hardly requires any effort to understand—charts and graphs of group and individual performance are fixtures in many workplaces.

- Some feedback is tucked away in the heads of customers—or your head as a manager. No matter how inaccessible it may seem, if your people need it to keep their performance on track, you need to get it to them, preferably while it's fresh and before it has been homogenized.

Display Feedback

Somebody once said that if it wasn't for all the statistics, baseball would have died years ago. True or not of baseball, it says something important about human nature. We love performance data—the more tangible, visible, and countable the better. How high did he jump? How far did it travel? How fast did she run? Questions like these hold endless fascination for us all.

In business, we track calls handled per hour or day, problems resolved on first contact, shipments per day, on-time deliveries against standard, and customers per register. Such feedback can be addictive. We love to know how we did all that today compared to yesterday, this month compared to last, in our department compared to a group in another building, or the people on another shift, or from another organization.

Through charts and graphs—the kind a normal human can decipher at a glance, not the multidimensional variety that requires a PhD in statistics to make sense of—data displays give employees valuable feedback on their performance and motivate them through the mechanisms of "confirm" and "correct."

Tom Connellan is a leading authority on the use of feedback, recognition, and reward systems in maintaining high levels of quality service. In his book, *Bringing Out the Best in Others!,* he identifies the six principles that the best display feedback systems follow:

1. *Feedback works best when given in relation to a specific service quality goal.* Goal-directed behavior is very

powerful behavior. Tell a new waiter or waitress that they waited on twenty customers tonight and the first question you'll hear is invariably, "Is that good?" Good feedback tells employees not only how they are doing, but how they are doing relative to the goals and performance standards they are expected to meet.

2. *Wherever possible, the feedback system should be managed by the people whose work created the service in the first place: frontline employees.* How many times do we put a staff rather than line person in charge of gathering, sorting, synthesizing, and circulating information on everything from delivery time, widget quality, and scrap, to customer satisfaction and employee retention? The net result is that by the time such staff-managed information gets back to where it can actually affect the service delivery system and process, it's almost always useless as either confirmation or correction.

Given the right tools and a little training, frontline employees should be quite capable of gathering information on their own performance, putting it in a PowerPoint chart or graph, matching it against predetermined norms, and deciding whether or not improvement is called for. And when they do it themselves, they are more likely to believe the data, will act on it faster, and will become more responsive to customers' unique needs because now they know "how they add up."

3. *Feedback should be immediate and should be collected and reported as soon after the completion of the service rendered as possible.* The sooner the feedback is received by the people it concerns most—the people it's about—the easier it is for them to relate their specific job behaviors to the customer's service quality or satisfaction assessment. If you were a driving instructor, you wouldn't wait until tomorrow to tell Peggy she just turned the wrong way on a one-way street. You'd want her to know how she is doing in time to keep you both from becoming someone else's statistics.

4. *Feedback should go to the person or team performing the job, not to the vice president in charge of boxes on surveys.* Obvious? Maybe. But check your current feedback practices.

How long will it take for information gathered today to reach the people at the front line? Rule of thumb: the older the data, the less useful for changing the way things get done in your service delivery system.

Let's suppose you just now decided to order four giant pepperoni pizzas as a lunch treat for the folks in your call center. How well received will your little gesture be if first the pizzas had to be signed for by a security guard two buildings away, then picked up by a mail clerk on regular office rounds, and then brought to your office for your signature before you could take them out to where you wanted them to go in the first place? How good will those pizzas taste by that time? And will you really want to be their bearer?

If Domino's and Pizza Hut can deliver direct, your feedback system can, too. Immediate, direct feedback helps your people meet their goals and targets, in the process minimizing the amount of "looking over their shoulder" corrective supervising you have to do. Remember, autonomy and self-reliance are key components of an environment that nurtures empowered frontline workers.

5. *After it has served its immediate purpose, relevant feedback should go to all levels of the organization.* Everyone has a "need to know" when it comes to information about how the organization is performing. But just because it's "feedback" doesn't mean it's feedback in the proper form or context. Senior management likely has no need for the level of detail that frontline employees and managers need to have to fine-tune the delivery system.

Asking "Who is this information relevant to?" instead of "Who would probably want to have a look at this?" is a good tool for eliminating needless paper shuffling. And the lower the proportion of useless information people see, the more attention they'll pay to information of value.

6. *Feedback should be graphically displayed.* The adage that "one picture is worth a thousand words" is certainly relevant when it comes to feedback. With the design capabilities and user-friendliness of today's software, it's easier to create compelling charts and graphs that give employees both the big

picture and snapshot-sharp specifics at the same time. It also provides a readily understandable comparative benchmark for the next batch of information.

Do your people really want to know? Believe it! We learned that lesson at the same theme park we mentioned earlier. According to the folks in the marketing department—who had been keeping all of the info to themselves—there were wild day-to-day variations in guest satisfaction. After much deliberation, it was decided that "something needed to be done."

But what? After discussing good and bad feedback methods with us, John, the human resources manager, had a fifty-foot-long by ten-foot-high wall next to the time clock turned into a giant graph for displaying guest satisfaction scores as measured by a thirty-six-item survey. Instead of batch-processing data, new survey results were added every day.

The meaning of the moving line was not lost on employees. In fact, in short order they began to ask for more detailed survey results so they could see exactly *where* improvement was needed. After a few weeks, the "guest satisfaction index" began rising. And though it took occasional dips, the wild swings in customer satisfaction were never seen again.

Troubleshooting Your Display Feedback System

When a feedback system doesn't work, it's often because the information gathered is being used incorrectly. It has stopped being feedback and has become a chore, a threat, or something to be avoided. Dr. Karen Brethower, an industrial psychologist, uses the following six questions for troubleshooting a sick feedback system.

1. *Is the feedback being used to embarrass, punish, or scold employees?* In one company, a "Rude Hog" award for the service rep with the lowest customer satisfaction ratings became a badge of honor. "Way to go Harry! Don't let the SOBs push you around" was the spirit it inspired.

2. *Is the feedback about something that has no payoff for the people receiving the information?* If there is no personal or departmental relevance to the information being collected, stop collecting it. Or at least file it under "nonessential."

3. *Is the information being provided too late for employees to act on it?* Too many things change too quickly for weeks-old or months-old information to have an effect on meaningful responses. You want to avoid giving people results from a customer satisfaction survey done six months ago.

4. *Is the feedback about something the people receiving it cannot change or affect?* You can tell a five-foot-tall person he's short, but nothing positive will come of it. Similarly, customers might report being upset about what it cost them in gas to drive to your store, but there's little your staff can do about it.

5. *Is the feedback about the wrong things?* Salespeople can't help it if customers think the store is inconveniently located or isn't decorated in a warm and friendly way. Get that feedback to someone who can act on it.

6. *Is the information difficult to collect and record?* Collecting and recording data can be a positive experience for your frontline people—unless the procedures are hellaciously difficult. We know of one company where employees rebelled against a quality improvement plan because they found the procedures so time-consuming that they were working overtime just to do their "real" jobs.

Good feedback is like a compass needle. It won't get you where you're going, but it will keep you pointed in the right direction.

> Good management consists of showing average people how to do the work of superior people.
>
> —John D. Rockefeller

25

The Art of Interpersonal Feedback

People remember best those things they discover,
learn and experience themselves. The only way you
help someone accept an idea as his own is to ask a
question and let him give the answer back to you.

—Dorothy Leeds

"How am I doing?" questions often have answers that can't be
meaningfully transferred to PowerPoint presentations or
graphs on the wall. Interpersonal feedback is the face-to-face,
manager-to-employee variation that is indispensable to an employee's morale, improvement, and growth. Mastering this vital part of your job takes courage, a good grasp of the human
psyche, and an overriding belief that coaching is an integral
rather than a peripheral function of your role as a manager.

As with "display" feedback, interpersonal feedback
comes in a variety of forms:

- Some will be based on your *opinions* or point of view
  regarding employees' performances.
- Some will be based on *standards*—more formal measures and efforts that define quality performance.

Standards, in turn, come in different styles. They can be:

- Written policies or rules: "Speed limit: 65 mph."
- Unwritten but generally accepted norms: "No swimsuits worn to the office."
- Specifically negotiated between you and your employees: "For the next ninety days, we need complete data in this format on the fifteenth of each month."

Which is better: feedback based on opinions or feedback based on standards? Either. Both. However, as you might imagine, feedback based on your opinion or point of view is much more likely to be challenged by your employees, especially if they do not agree with the feedback.

- When the patrol officer tells you that you were clocked on the radar doing 82.5 mph and you crossed a double yellow line when you passed a car, there are objective standards behind the feedback.
- But if you are stopped for "reckless driving," your judgment may be quite different than the officer's.

Whenever possible, work to coach from performance standards. They are agreed upon up front and should be well known to your employees. Your people will be more receptive to coaching based on concrete standards rather than on opinion or personal preference.

Ensuring That Feedback Is Heard

The goal of providing feedback is to have it "take"—that is, making sure it is heard, valued, and hopefully used by the employee to continue or improve performance. As a supervisor, you want *all* of your comments to matter. You know how to generate the information. But how do you improve your chances of having your people accept and act on it?

If you give feedback in a stern, parental way, you may encounter resistance because of the way your manner and tone remind people, who are adults, of a very strict parent. By the same token, if you give feedback in an off-hand, flippant, "no big deal" way, employees will be inclined to view it as just that: "no big deal." The way you look and sound to your staff affects how they hear, accept, and act on your message.

Two approaches can help:

1. *Work from personal expertise.* If people respect your skill and knowledge in the area on which you are giving feedback, they're more likely to give it serious consideration, even if they disagree or feel defensive. Joe Wannabee's over-the-fence feedback on how to improve your driveway jump shot—which you think is a game-winner—is easy to laugh off and ignore. But if your neighbor happens to be Lebron James, you'll probably give the feedback some serious thought.

2. *Work from performance standards.* You can't compel your employees to respect your expertise. However, you can increase their receptivity to corrective feedback by basing it on standards whenever possible. This takes planning. You can't announce a new standard or expectation and then immediately critique performance against it. Employees need a clear understanding of your expectations and standards. They also need time to work up to those levels. Make sure standards are set early and are clearly understood if you're going to rely on them for corrective action.

Feedback must be specific and actionable to be of any value. General comments like "your attitude needs improving" or "you need to listen better to your callers" will only frustrate employees because they won't know what to do with it. Instead you might say, "I've noticed that you haven't been using the recovery process we've been stressing in our team meetings when you deal with upset customers. Apologizing is an important part of making sure customers who have problems go away happy, regardless of who is to blame. Can you help me understand why you haven't been using that part of the process?"

Giving actionable feedback often starts with asking good questions—the best advice givers are usually the best listeners. And good listeners are invariably good question askers.

"John, I had a call from Mr. Sanchez. He's been a valued customer over the years, and I'd like us to help him if we can. He was a little upset with his last conversation with you. So I need to understand what this is all about. Could you summarize the situation for me?"

Mr. Sanchez, it turns out, wanted some additional time to make a payment and didn't care much for John's response, which essentially stated company policy.

Manager/coach: "What alternatives do you think the customer would have been able to accept in this situation?"

Once you've explored options with John, you can help him select the next step. "It sounds like there are a couple of alternatives you can offer him. Which one do you want to propose first?"

Open-ended questions are generally more useful for coaching scenarios than the close-ended variety. Some examples include:

"What was the customer upset about?
"What have you tried so far?"
"What can I do to help?"
"What would you like to accomplish when you call her back?"
"How do you think you might plan your work more effectively?"

Giving Clear Feedback

Here are six steps to help you plan clear feedback:

1. Specify what the task is and why it is important to the unit or team. Discuss both the benefit to the team or unit if the task is accomplished well and the consequences to the unit or team if it is not.
2. Determine what other work is currently being done and mutually agree on how improvement efforts in this area rank in priority to other tasks or responsibilities. Customer contact employees usually have plenty on

their plates, and providing guidance on which tasks or goals you see as the most critical can help bring a sense of order to their multitasking.

3. Agree on a standard. Make sure it covers all elements of the task, such as completion time, quality expected, and quantity expected, and decide which element is most important.

4. Discuss the resources (time and materials) needed for the task and agree on what actions should be taken to meet these requirements.

5. Discuss: (1) what you believe a person would need to know and be able to do in order to do the task well, (2) your view of the individual employee's abilities, and (3) the employee's self-assessment of task and abilities. This is important. You may learn that an employee doesn't possess the necessary skill or knowledge to accomplish a task or meet a service standard, and some additional training or coaching will be needed.

6. In concert with the employee, jointly establish the methods to be used to monitor progress, solve problems related to the task, and evaluate the final result.

Feedback is the breakfast, lunch, and dinner of champions because it feeds growth and success. Winners like to hear plenty of "you're the greatest" confirming feedback. Winners also know that getting better comes with feedback that helps them see their performance in the context of long-term goals.

Good feedback takes effective planning. It becomes more effective and powerful the more it is sincerely given and is based on clear expectations and standards. And like breakfast, lunch, and dinner, you need to provide it on a regular basis.

The wise leader does not try to protect people from themselves. The light of awareness shines equally on what is pleasant and on what is not pleasant.

—John Heider
The Tao of Leadership

26

Incenting Great Service

Give the world the best that you have, and the best will come back to you.

—Madeline Bridges

The service tech at an auto dealership programs in new car customers' radio stations from their trade-in and lets them discover it. A Hertz courtesy van driver gets renters to shout in unison "I love Hertz" on their way to the airport after car turn-in. A front desk manager at a hotel in Orlando installed steps in front of the check-in counter so children could "check in" beside their parents.

Great service not only means service providers rewarding a different type of behavior, it means making the new reward match the new requirement. The bottom line is that great service requires rewarding excellence. The following are five principles of great service incentives.

1. *Match the tone of service.* Great service at a hospital looks, sounds, and feels very different from the same service delivered at a theme park or a funeral home. The incentive needs to fit the tone and ambiance of the context in which it is delivered. Recognition at Walt Disney World always contains a bit of pixie dust— Mickey's magic. Recognition at the classy Sewell

Lexus dealership in Dallas happens at a black tie dinner at a five-star hotel complete with overnight accommodations for the award recipients and their spouse or partner. Netflix uses their Friday potluck lunches to recognize employees, reinforcing the informal attitude and friendliness of their service experience.

2. *Recognize individuals and the team.* Great service often requires great teamwork. Marriott's Gold Coin program focuses on involving the customer in identifying a "front of the house" associate who delivered remarkable service. But, the program has a special twist. A guest is given a gold coin at check-in with instructions to give the coin to anyone who delivers great service. The gold coin recipient then identifies a "back-of-the-house" associate who helped the recipient deliver great service; both get recognized.

3. *Link to the customer.* A major hotel used a creative approach to service that made guests feel that they witnessed magic. When a guest arrived, the doorman asked the customer if he or she was a returning guest. If the guest said "yes," as the doorman brought the customer's luggage to the front desk, he or she sent an "ear pull" signal to the front desk clerk who greeted the customer with "welcome back." The "ear pull" signal was then passed to the bellman who escorted the guest to the room. The result? The hotel started the chain link award. People in the "ear pull" chain who received acknowledgment from the guest on a comment card were given a chain link with their name engraved to be placed on a chain that got longer each quarter a link was awarded.

4. *Affirm responsible freedom.* Great customer service typically involves breaking patterns and abandoning "the way we've always done it." To get service creativity, it is important to affirm appropriate risk taking—not foolhardy recklessness, but employees who couple service with stewardship—taking care of the customer while taking care of the organization. One high-tech

company gives its annual "green weenie" award to the individual who, while clearly pursuing excellence, made a mistake that produced the greatest organizational learning and improvement.

5. *Value outcomes, not just the experience.* A happy-go-lucky nurse won the hearts of her patients by bringing them flowers grown in her garden and cookies baked in her oven. They raved to managers about her sunny disposition and special generosity. She was the recipient of a special recognition at the annual awards banquet to the sharp displeasure of her coworkers. While all acknowledged her special way with patients, they were quick to point out her sloppy paperwork, inconsistent hand washing, and unwillingness to pull her weight on tasks they all shared. All those poor practices adversely impacted the health care outcome, but were out of sight of her adoring fans. Effective recognition practices require performance on "the basics" to be at least at expected levels. We all enjoy friendly flight attendants, but the plane must still land in the right city!

Great service is a handmade surprise tailored to the receiver. Its power to attract and retain customers lies in its capacity to make customers feel they have been bestowed a valuable expression that honors the very nobility of service. Its originality and imagination telegraph an innate commitment to excellence. Great service requires incentives with a creative twist. However, the goal is not an incentive that simply affirms; it is one that channels energy and directs practices that result in customer loyalty.

> People may take a job for more money, but they often leave it for more recognition.
>
> —Bob Nelson

27

Celebrate Success

I have yet to find the man, however exalted his station,
who did not do better work and put forth greater effort
under a spirit of approval than under a spirit of criticism.

—Charles Schwab

Celebration serves a variety of functions in an organization.
On the simplest level, it is a form of recognition and reward.
That, in and of itself, is an important function and a worthy
purpose.

But celebration is also a way of nourishing group spirit. It
represents a moment in time when a glimpse of a transformed
organization—a product of the efforts of people from many
levels—can be seen, felt, and enjoyed. In truly human terms,
celebration reaffirms to people that they are an important part
of something that really matters.

For most people, the feeling of being part of something
important and meaningful is a powerful motivator. Being part
of a winning team, being seen as the best in the industry, and
achieving something others admire and respect hold a power
that can make salary increases, bonuses, generous 401K plans,
and even the most carefully designed perk program seem lack-
luster by comparison.

Celebration reminds everyone that purposes and goals not
only exist, but are exciting, important, and attainable.
Reconfirming to people at all levels in your organization that
they are part of something important, that the service they

provide is vital to both the organization and the people they serve, may be the most important motivational principle of all.

Celebration should be an integral part of the way you recognize and reward good performance. To make it effective, pay attention to *when* you celebrate, *why* you celebrate, with *whom* you celebrate, and *how* you celebrate.

When

Timing is a key variable in a multitude of service activities, and celebration is no exception. As with other forms of reinforcement, "the quicker the better" is one good rule of thumb. It's hard for people to get realistically happy in December over something they did last June. Following are some good times to celebrate.

1. *When you need to mark the end of a project or major effort.* Achievers (those who take pride in a job well done) often have a need for closure and the knowledge that their efforts have led to a visible conclusion. When the work just goes on and on, lack of closure can burn them out. Achievers need to know they've achieved, in other words. In the absence of natural closure, invent it: "Fifty days without . . . , " "Three quarters in a row during which we . . . , " or "The 10th (100th?) positive customer letter."

2. *When you are making a transition from one stage to another.* Celebration can not only mark the end of one phase, it can acknowledge the beginning of a new one, reinforcing new goals and standards with the recognition that the last ones proved eminently doable.

3. *When your unit has met an important goal.* Whether short term or long term, goals achieved in business should be like goals scored in a soccer or hockey game: an occasion for a few immediate "high fives" before the game resumes in earnest. If you meet monthly targets for resolving customer problems on first contact or

quarterly goals for on-time deliveries, celebrate with something beyond a "nice job" for the troops. Spontaneity is as important in celebrating as planning. Sometimes you'll have the champagne on ice. Other times, you'll just want to savor the unexpected moment in whatever way seems best at the time.

Why

Picking your spots is important. So, too, is having a reason for the celebration. Without a strategic component, celebrations can become trivialized or wind up reinforcing the wrong things. Following are some good reasons to celebrate.

1. *To motivate.* Celebrating obviously lends passion to the rational, emotion to the logical, and joy to the somber. It rekindles the spirit and leaves a warm glow that can endure long after the moment has passed. It pumps air back into the organizational balloon.
2. *To model.* Celebrations create a forum or setting that can be used to tell the stories of new service heroes. By making good examples of your people, others on the service team gain a deeper understanding of the attitudes and actions you want them to emulate.
3. *To communicate priorities.* Just as what gets rewarded gets repeated, what you decide to celebrate showcases your priorities. If the reasons you select involve cost-cutting, budget-reducing, and general frugality, your people will know to pinch pennies. In contrast, if service excellence is the consistent theme, you'll make it very clear that working for customers is at the top of your list.
4. *To encourage.* Sales organizations know the value of motivational sales rallies that renew the spirit of people whose job entails hearing no in every variation known to man (and woman). Service people endure similar stresses, and often without the counterbalance of sales successes. Celebrations help recharge service batteries drawn down by the emotional labor of dealing with difficult customers.

Who

Celebrations are for people, by people. The human element has many dimensions, including those that follow.

1. *Your Role as Manager.* This is one occasion where it's better to lead than delegate. Sure, it's important to get others involved. But you miss an important and necessary opportunity and can actually send the wrong message by taking an "I'll just stay here in the background" position. You do not have to be a charismatic, back-slapping cheerleader type to lead the effort. Be yourself, but be up front—that's how your people know the celebration is truly meaningful to you.

2. *Their Role as Participants.* Basically, the more the better. There are times for small, intimate gatherings of a chosen few. But times of celebration aren't among them. Err on the side of too many people rather than too few. Let everyone bask in the warmth of success.

3. *The Prominence of Contributors.* Involve everyone who contributed in the cause for celebration. The key word is "contributed." You don't want to muddy the celebratory waters by giving credit to people where none is due, but you also don't want to recognize only a few of the many who played a part. It's even worth the risk of an Oscar night marathon. For recipients, the chance to be acknowledged and to use their "moment in the sun" to acknowledge those who contributed to their achievements outweighs where the big and little hands are on the clock.

4. *The Appearance of Special Guests.* You compliment your people and your guests when you reinforce the importance of the celebration by inviting others. Consider including a few key customers or vendors, or people from another department on which your people rely. A caveat: Defer to the feelings of the celebrants in bringing in outsiders—the unexpected appearance of someone they have good reason to label a "customer from hell" can throw cold water in their faces.

How

There's no one right way to celebrate. In fact, try to explore different forms of celebration to keep things from becoming routine and predictable. (You can, to be sure, have worse problems than getting yourself into a "celebrations rut" because of your continuing stream of successes.) Here are a few guidelines.

1. *Keep it upbeat.* Celebrations should be fun, they should be positive in nature, and they should avoid things your celebrants find boring (such as the shopworn "chicken-a-la-Goodyear" meal and attendant boring speeches and bad jokes). Make the event festive and fun. Get lots of ideas by getting lots of people involved in the planning and execution.
2. *Use lasting symbols.* Find tangible ways to preserve the moment: hats and t-shirts, banners, a video that tells the story (or, better yet, lets those who did the deed tell the story), a write-up in internal publications, special plaques, or keepsakes.
3. *Make it classy.* Aim for celebrations that are public, not private; open, not closed; spontaneous, not scheduled to the minute; and inclusive, not elitist. They should reflect organizational values from start to finish.
4. *Recognize and reward.* Pull the celebration together around the people and the achievements you're recognizing. Otherwise, it's just another party.

Some Noteworthy Celebrations

• At Netflix, the online DVD subscription service based in Los Gatos, California, managers celebrate hitting targets for new subscribers to the company's "Friends" network, which gives customers a glimpse at how their friends have reviewed movies they've seen, with Friday afternoon potluck lunches. Managers publicly thank all those who had a hand in achieving the goal, and employees have a chance to socialize and sample creative dishes their colleagues have cooked up.

- Hartsfield–Jackson Atlanta International Airport throws an annual celebration recognizing the outstanding efforts by airport personnel—encompassing all airlines and other airport services. Winners' stories are shared, and tales range from assisting a pregnant woman give birth in an airport restroom, to ensuring children get on the right flight, to going the extra mile ensuring a passenger gets the individualized care he or she requires. Prizes include plaques, dinner gift certificates, high-definition televisions, trips, and even a new car. It is a day filled with fun, frivolity, and inspiration.

- At LensCrafters, they celebrate the end of a store-level sales contest in a unique fashion. The awards meeting starts in a familiar way. Performance awards are passed out, customer compliment letters are read aloud, and individual employees are saluted by the regional manager. As the meeting winds to a close, however, a unique (and greatly anticipated) twist occurs. The individual with the best contest record closes the meeting by serving up a cream pie straight into the mug of a designated recipient—point blank, no ducking, no begging off—whoop!

Don't ask. Some organizational traditions and symbols aren't meant to be understood by outsiders.

> The more you praise and celebrate your life, the more there is in life to celebrate.
>
> —Oprah Winfrey

Imperative 8

Set the Tone and Lead the Way

It's sometimes hard to believe that you have any "power" over anyone in your organization. Or that very much of what you say, let alone what you do, has much influence over other people's behavior. But looks can be deceiving.

The people who think of you as "the boss" are more than a little swayed by your actions. Like it or not, you are the personal role model for many of the people who work for you. How they see you deal with and talk about peers, colleagues, employees, and customers tells them what the real rules of conduct are for your part of the organization.

You can't con or manipulate people into doing quality work or caring about their customers. You *can* lead them there. Your personal example of doing things right, of taking the time to listen to customers and employees with patience, and focusing your

energy on things that say "quality service" to your customers—
internal and external—are critical parts of your leadership role.
You, through your day-to-day example and leadership, set the
tone and lead the way.

> If you are serious about product quality and customer
> service, and you're not spending 35 percent of your
> time on it (by gross calendar analysis), then you are not
> serious about it.
>
> —Tom Peters
> Management guru

28

Great Service Leaders Foster Trust

The best way to find out if you can trust somebody is to trust them.

—Ernest Hemingway

We all live our lives on promises. From the time a child can grasp the concept of "cross my heart and hope to die," there is a forever realization that anxiety can be only reduced through proof of trust while waiting for a promise to be kept. From "scout's honor" to "I do" to "the whole truth and nothing but the truth," we seek cues that allay our worries. Lifeguards, the bus schedule, and the spotlessness of a hospital room are all obvious artifacts of promises waiting to be kept.

All service begins with a trust gap, the emotional space between hope and evidence, between expectation and fulfillment. Service begins with a promise made or implied: "We'll be landing on time," "It will be ready by noon," or "Your order will be right out." Granted, great service recovery can transform an aggrieved customer into a satisfied customer, but the residue of betrayal will leave a disappointed customer perpetually on guard for the time when letdown reoccurs.

Trust is the emotion that propels customers to the other side of the gap between expectation and experience. The manner in which a person, unit, or organization manages the trust gap drives every other component of the service encounter.

The manner in which a person, unit, or organization capitalizes on the trust gap takes a service given to a service gift.

As customers, our journey across the high wire of faith is a trip with or without anguish depending on how strong the net of trust is that the service provider has put there to support our passage. Customers' perception of that "net of trust" makes all the difference in how they grade their experiences. No net, no loyalty; shaky net, no loyalty. And, smart organizations—those that retain the best customers for the longest time—understand that managing the trust gap can never be taken for granted. They know that customer trust must always be treated as a fragile bond, as if it can be shattered with a single malfunction, misunderstanding, or mishap. It is the most important component of a leader's role in a service organization.

Trust Ensues from Optimistic Leaders

Parents who seek to have their children proceed into the world with confidence and trust typically communicate optimism. "Look on the brighter side," "It not as bad as you think," and "It will all be better in the morning" were the kind of phrases most people heard growing up. They were usually delivered by an optimistic parent to an anxious child after a scary moment or dream. They also were normally the precursor to calm, confidence, and trust.

Great leaders who seek to create an atmosphere of trust are optimistic about their world and their associates. Optimism does not imply a Pollyannaish attitude or blind desire. It does, however, mean courageous hope and rock solid conviction in one's capacity to negotiate troubled waters with unexpected twists and dangerous turns. Leaders who foster trust in relationships have a clear idea of what the relationship ought to be like. They also are quick to give early forewarning of that expectation. They are ever vigilant for evidence that their expectations will be realized or thwarted. They enter relationships with optimism, hope, and conviction that all will go well. Great service leaders ground their optimism in a belief that cracks can be filled and repaired by their will and the power of the special relationship. Best does not mean always perfect. The quest is to trust service employees, service leaders, and customers to always be striving for the best. And without at least some level of that trust and belief, true success is rarely possible.

Trust Requires Honest Leaders

Great service leaders who seek a trusting climate work diligently to always assert the truth. This proactive gesture keeps integrity at the forefront of all dealings. "One of the surest signs of a bad or declining relationship is the absence of complaints. Nobody is ever THAT satisfied, especially not over an extended period of time. The person is either not being candid or not being contacted." These words of Harvard professor and marketing guru, Ted Levitt, were written about customers in his classic *Harvard Business Review* article, "After the Sale Is Over . . . ." They could just as easily be about all relationships. The absence of unabashed candor reflects the decline of trust and the deterioration of the relationship.

Ask anybody what they believe to be the number one cause of divorce. After a few cute answers like "marriage," eight in ten will tell you "lack of communication." A key part of special and important relationships is straight talk—a two-way pursuit of truth. No relationship is likely to be perfect all the time. The healthy work relationship, like the healthy marriage, is marked by candor and welcomed critique. Honesty fuels more honesty if defensiveness is absent. And as candor triggers improvement, those who serve feel responsive, those served feel heard, and the relationship emerges with greater health.

Trust Happens through Leader Respect

Respect is made of admiration and honor. When we respect someone, it means we admire who they are and/or what they do. There is either an "I wish I could . . . like they can" type of awe or an "I know how hard it is to . . ." type of connection. Honor is also made of esteem. To esteem a relationship is to ascribe credit or adoration to it. It involves seeking ways to bring accolades and praise to the relationship.

Riverside Health Care in Newport News, Virginia, experienced a major loss in 2002. Education manager Jean Raines unexpectedly passed away. Most organizations annually experience the loss of a special employee. This particular loss was uniquely challenging. It was not that people thought Jean would be there forever. She had already worked more than forty years for Riverside. It was the fact that Jean honored the people who worked around her.

Jean Raines did more than pass out accolades or attaboys. She visibly demonstrated her devotion for her associates. She nurtured, celebrated, remembered, teased, affirmed, and supported. At her standing room only funeral, Riverside president Caroline Martin described Jean this way: "She honored *all* of us by the way she showed her abiding love for *each* of us." Adequate leaders show a love for their work. Good leaders show a love for their organization. Great leaders show "an abiding love for each of us."

Trust Comes from Keeping Promises

Reliability is the foundation of trust; trust is the glue of special relationships. Keeping promises is about protecting the sacredness of commitments. It is about caring enough to remember. "Relationships live or die by promises kept," says Marcia Corbett of CLG, Inc. "Reliability is the foundation of mutual trust," advises Carlo Medici, president and general manager of Bracco Diagnostics in Princeton, New Jersey. "It is being able to meet every promise every time."

"You are only as good as your word," was advice you likely heard growing up. "A person's word is his bond," you probably read. All these old maxims match Texas A&M professor Len Berry's service quality research that affirms that the number one attribute of service from the customer's perspective is reliability—do you keep your promises? The research on leaders' relationships with associates is equally convincing.

We commonly use the word "natural" to refer to things that are pure or organic, meaning no bad stuff added. We also use it to mean innate or native, as in one's natural talent. Great service requires leadership that reflects a purity of purpose as well as an instinct in practice. It does not mean leadership cannot be learned or refined. It does mean magnetic service leadership draws on the genetic material of human relationships that is as untainted as children at play and as wholesome as a family sharing a special moment.

> Trust is the glue of life. It's the most essential ingredient in effective communication. It's the foundational principle that holds all relationships.
>
> —Stephen R. Covey

29

Great Service Leadership in Action

The first responsibility of a leader is to define reality. The last is to say thank you. In between, the leader is a servant.

—Max DePree
author of *Leadership Is an Art*

It all started with an exercise at an executive retreat. We had been queried by participants throughout the session to reveal what "walking the talk" looked like for a service leader.

"Sure, we're supposed to be role models. We know all about making service excellence a priority and how we need to communicate the service vision," they chided. "But, that's just consultant talk. What does 'being a service leader' look like up close on a Monday morning when all heck breaks loose in the call center or on the sales floor?"

Remembering the lessons from Consulting 101, we chose a small group exercise as a way of answering the question. "Assume you implemented today a new unconditional service guarantee," we instructed the group. "The service guarantee promised that if customers were not completely happy with the service experience—how they were treated—they would get a refund equal to ten times the price paid for the product or service. What actions would you take to avoid quickly going bankrupt?"

The mood in the room shifted from skepticism to feverish brainstorming. Even the quieter members began filling up flipcharts with leader actions aimed at keeping the service spirit alive and employees focused on taking care of customers. When the exercise was completed, the twelve managers had generated over 100 specific "Monday morning" actions. And in the process, they discovered their own answers to the "walking the talk" question.

We compared their list against what we have witnessed from leaders known for inspiring, instigating, and sustaining a culture famous for service. Some have names that identify their enterprise—Bruce Nordstrom, Michael Dell, and Bill Marriott. Others are known only to their associates, stockholders, and customers. Their actions have similar themes.

They Connect

Leader connections with energy are those laced with authenticity. First Bank and Trust, headquartered in Lubbock, Texas, once had a policy allowing a loan officer who had a loan that exceeded his or her lending limit to get it approved simply by getting another loan officer with a higher lending authority to sign the loan. The policy was changed to one that required the loan committee, not just another loan officer, to approve all loans that exceeded a loan officer's lending authority.

An important loan to the bank was sent to bank CEO Barry Orr for approval when it exceeded a particular lending officer's authority. Barry signed the loan for the originating loan officer, believing at the time his signature was enough approval. When an employee in the loan department boldly challenged the CEO for not following the new loan policy guidelines, he emailed her, curtly stating that he was confident he had the authority—as CEO—to approve the loan. Courageously, she emailed back: "According to our new loan policy, you do not. It must go to loan committee." When Barry realized she was correct, he emailed her an apology, acknowledged his error, thanked her for challenging him, and copied every employee involved. But he did not stop there. He stopped by her desk to personally apologize.

Effective service leaders avoid getting "stuck in meetings." Try to schedule a sit down meeting with Larry Kurzweil, president of Universal Studios Hollywood, and you're likely to hear, "Sure we can meet. You don't mind if we walk the park while we talk, do you?" Kurzweil's attentive listening is punctuated with stops to ask questions of associates or give directions to guests. It's almost like Universal runs on Larry's supercharged battery and if he's not out there meeting, greeting, and energizing, the park will deflate and go flat. Being visible, making yourself available to answer staff questions, pitching in to serve customers during busy times, and opting to communicate face to face rather than relying on e-mail whenever possible all help foster trust by creating the sense you're working alongside the troops, not tucked safely away in a "management-only" bunker far from the action.

They Support

In the past, service leadership meant control and consistency. The "boss" of yesteryear kept a tight rein; otherwise, employees would "get lazy and fail to work." We know now that employees act like adults when they are treated like adults. Employees who manage a tight personal budget, buy and sell real estate, and prepare complex tax returns, not to mention successfully juggle schedules filled with soccer games, dentist appointments, or part-time college classes, likely have the wisdom and experience to handle almost any work assignment. At home, they don't need anyone ensuring they're "empowered" or have "appropriate supervision."

The service leader's role is to support and serve employees. That means running interference and getting people the resources they need so they can consistently work at a high level; it also means supporting and coaching them—not just assigning blame—when they've had difficult interactions with upset or insensitive customers.

As a service leader, you're still in charge of control and consistency, of course. But it's a goal you pursue *with* employees, not something you *impose* on them. If your people are clear on unit and organizational goals, if they know what's expected to accomplish service standards and norms, and if they understand the "whys" behind all those objectives, they will help you ensure control and consistency if allowed. Effective leaders always look for ways to involve, include, and invite their employees in service delivery.

They Listen

Knowing that listening to your people is important and *being* a good listener are two very different things. Ask employees about the listening skills of their bosses and most will give them a failing grade. Why is it that with an infinite number of books and articles written on the topic employees continue to ding their leaders on their listening skills? We think the problem has less to do with *communication* management and much more to do with *noise* management.

Most leaders *can* be great listeners. Let their seven-year-old come crying about a neighborhood conflict and you will see great listening. Zero in on a corner conversation they're having in a funeral home during the wake of a friend and you will see great listening. Yet mix the normal pace and chaos of a work day with the typical "I'm the boss" persona—and the mindset that "employees don't need to be babied"—and you have a prescription for the just-get-to-the-punch-line type of listening we see with too many leaders.

The sounds of great listening tell us that effective listeners don't start doing anything special, but they do stop doing something normal—they don't even attempt to listen when they know they can't provide undivided attention. "Hold my calls," "Let's get out of here so we can really talk," or "Tell him I'll have to call back" are words that telegraph noise management. They say to employees, "What you have to say is so important, I don't want to miss a word." If you can't give your people that kind of focus, postpone the encounter until you can. It's better to say, "Tom, I want to give you my complete attention, but I'm an hour from a crucial meeting and I would honestly only be giving you half of my attention. Can we schedule this later today when I can really focus?" Then make sure you live up to that promise.

A wise leader once said, "There are no individuals at work who are more important to your success than your employees . . . not your boss, not your customers, not your vendors." Make sure your listening practices reflect that truism.

They Enrich

"Add value to every moment by taking it personal," was the advice we heard Greg Haller, president of the West Area for Verizon Wireless, give to associates at an employee rally. The words come from a man renowned for his passion for customer service. Great service leaders always look for small ways to add value; instead of barking an order or sending an e-mail directive, they inspire by telling a story of how someone in the organization thrilled a customer by quickly or creatively resolving a tough problem. Instead of determining how well the organization is serving customers by reading customer satisfaction reports, they get out on the front lines and find out face to face, talking to customer contact employees and interacting with clients. They abhor excuses, blame, or any actions that acquiesce to the status quo rather than altering it in the name of improved service.

Your people—your followers—take their cue from you. You influence how they feel about the organization as a whole, about your unit in particular, about the type of work they do, about customers, and about themselves. What you value, they will value. While that may seem a heavy burden to bear, setting the tone and modeling good service behaviors are the very essence of being a good leader.

They Inspire

Don Freeman, chairman of Freeman, speaks from "the heart instead of a chart" when he addresses his managers about taking the courageous step of changing the Freeman culture to one focused on building customer loyalty. A leading full-service contractor for expositions and conventions, Dallas-based Freeman has long delivered exemplary service to its key customers—those who manage and coordinate conventions and exhibitions. To grow the company, Freeman knew it would have to build an equally strong reputation with customers who exhibit at shows, not just show managers. In response to customer suggestions, Freeman opened a new customer support center as one way to do that. "Unlike some call centers where the primary purpose is to take orders, our center is designed to assist exhibitors with show service questions and quickly resolve their issues," says center manager Brenda McCord.

Don Freeman, like other effective service leaders, knows how important it is for leaders to set the mood, tone, and tenor of the company, buoy people's spirits, and enlist them in a cause. At the same time, he understands that few people want to work for a "cheerleader" boss—the kind of visionless manipulator who simply enjoys the sound of his own voice and the thrill of talking others into doing his bidding. People will volunteer to work for bosses, however, who are at their inspirational best during tough times, who model the behaviors they ask others to show with customers, and who take time to coach and support rather than berate or blame when things go awry on the front lines.

They Offer a Strategy of Optimism and Tenacity

The service quality journey is not always easy. In fact, it is often tough and discouraging. The new computer hardware or software you installed frustrates rather than helps. One of your most valuable customers tells you to take a hike after a less-than-model conversation with your most experienced and trusted employee. Two of your new hires simply stop showing up for work. And you learn that your unit will face a significant budget reduction in the next biennium. This is the time when effective leaders draw optimism and tenacity from their followers—and give it back tenfold.

Effective leaders know the wisdom of the maxim, "abandon all hope for a better yesterday." They lift spirits by always focusing on a better tomorrow, understanding the folly of dwelling on past mistakes or miscalculations. When the pressure is on and the stakes are high, effective service leaders also set the standard for their organizations. As any parent knows who has hammered a finger instead of a nail with an observant child present, modeling is most memorable and powerful when under pressure.

Great leaders connect, support, enrich, inspire, and provide hope. They also patiently listen to employees, customers, and vendors in a constant quest for service improvement. The bottom line is that great service leaders achieve that status because of one overriding quality: they *serve*.

> I find the great thing in this world is, not where we stand, but in what direction we are moving.
>
> —Oliver Wendell Holmes
> American Jurist

Endnotes

1. American Express, "Americans Will Spend 9% More with Companies That Provide Excellent Service," July 7, 2010, http://about.americanexpress.com/news/pr/2010/barometer.aspx (accessed October 29, 2010).
2. Lora Kolodny, "Study: 82% of U.S. Consumers Bail on Brands after Bad Customer Service," October 13, 2010, www.techcrunch.com.
3. Ron Zemke and Chip R. Bell, *Service Magic: The Art of Amazing Your Customers* (Dearborn, Mich. Dearborn Financial Publishing, 2003), p. 172.
4. Jena McGregor, "Putting Customers First," *Fast Company*, October 2004.
5. Richard L. Nolan and Suresh Kotha, "Harley-Davidson: Preparing for the Next Century," *Harvard Business Online*, March 14, 2006.
6. Benjamin Schneider and David E. Bowen, "Employee and Customer Perceptions of Service in Banks: Replication and Extension," *Journal of Applied Psychology*, 70(1985): 423-433.
7. Stanley Holmes and Wendy Zellner, "The Costco Way," *BusinessWeek*, April 12, 2004.
8. "Emerging Work Force Study," *BusinessWeek,* March 1, 1999, based on the research conducted by Charles Fishman.
9. John H. Fleming, Curt Coffman, and James K. Harter, "Managing Your Human Sigma," *Harvard Business Review*, July-August 2005.
10. Chip R. Bell and John R. Patterson, "Customer Service Dashboard," *Customer Relationship Management*, July 2006.
11. Lucas Conley, "Customer-Centered Leader: Maxine Clark," *Fast Company*, October 2005.
12. Courtesy of Convergys 2010 Customer Scorecard Research, www.convergys.com/research. Used with permission.
13. Ibid.
14. "Think Customers," The 1 to 1 Blog, http://www.1to1media.com/weblog/ (accessed October 21, 2010).

15. Ibid.
16. Lora Kolodny, "82% of U.S. Customers Bail on Brands after Bad Service," TechCrunch.com, October 13, 2010, http://techcrunch.com/2010/10/13/customer-service-rightnow/ (accessed October 23, 2012)
17. Courtesy of Convergys 2010 Customer Scorecard Research, www.convergys.com/research. Used with permission.
18. 2005 Respond Study, reported at Capturing Customer Feedback, Unica, The Marketers Consortium, http://unicashare.typepad.com/share/2006/10/capturing_custo.html (accessed December 8, 2010).
19. Zemke and Bell, p. 165.
20. John Blasberg, Vijay Vishwanath, and James Allen, "Tools for Converting Consumers into Advocates," *Strategy and Leadership,* March 1, 2008.
21. Karl Albrecht and Ron Zemke, *Service America!* (New York: McGraw-Hill Publications, 2002), p. 108.
22. Courtesy of Convergys 2010 Customer Scorecard Research, www.convergys.com/research. Used with permission.
23. Albert Mehrabian, *Silent Messages: Implicit Communication of Emotions and Attitudes* (Belmont, Calif. Wadsworth, 1981). Currently distributed by Albert Mehrabian, e-mail: am@kaaj.com.
24. Ibid.
25. Courtesy of Convergys 2010 Customer Scorecard Research, www.convergys.com/research. Used with permission.
26. Ibid.
27. Ibid.
28. Robert Spector, *Anytime, Anywhere: How the Best Bricks-and-Clicks Businesses Deliver Seamless Service to Their Customers* (New York: Perseus Publishing, 2002), p. 60.
29. Lisa Arthur, "Have No Fear, Let Customers Control Your Brand," Think Customers: The 1 to 1 Blog, September 12, 2010, http://www.1to1media.com/weblog/2010/09/guest_blogger_lisa_arthur_have.html (accessed October 11, 2010).

30. Mila D'Antonio, "Mountain Dew Hands Over Its Brand to Fans," *1to1 Magazine*, September 2010, http://www.1to1media.com/View.aspx?docid=32519. See also www.dewmocracymediahub.com.

31. Lisa Arthur, *op. cit.*

32. Ellen Davis, "eBay CEO Discusses Mobile, Customer Feedback and Embracing Competition," September 23, 2009, http://blog.shop.org/2009/09/23/ebay-ceo-discusses-mobile-customer-feedback-and-embracing-competition/.

33. See Marriott on the Move blog, http://www.blogs.marriott.com/.

34. Erick Schonfeld, "Forrester Forecast: Online Retail Sales Will Grow to $250B by 2014," www.techcrunch.com, March 8, 2010.

35. Ron Zemke and Chip R. Bell, *Service Magic: The Art of Amazing Your Customers* (Dearborn, Mich. Dearborn Financial Publishing, 2003), p. 165.

36. Jean M. Otte, corporate vice president of quality management, National Car Rental System, presentation to the MN Chapter, Society of Consumer Affairs Professionals in Business, June 8, 1992.

37. "2005 Customer Rage Study," Customer Care Alliance and the Center for Services Leadership, Arizona State University School of Business.

38. "Customer First Aware Profiles," *Fast Company,* October 2004.

39. Ron Zemke and Chip R. Bell, *Service Magic: The Art of Amazing Your Customers* (Dearborn, Mich. Dearborn Financial Publishing, 2003), p. 165.

40. "Customer First Aware Profiles," *Fast Company*, October 2004.

41. Michael A. Prospero, "Leading Listener: Cabela's," *Fast Company*, October 2005.

42. Jena McGregor, "Employee Innovator: USAA," *Fast Company*, October 2005.

Index

Adoption Metaphor
 (ADOPT), 142–143
"After the Sale is Over"
 (Levitt), 215
aggrieved customer
 customer emotional
  state, 132
 customer
  expectations,
  131
 effective planning
  and, 133
 frontline people and,
  132
 management and,
  130–131
 Smokescreen
  Principle, 132
Albrecht, Karl, 101
The Aquarian
 Conspiracy
 (Ferguson), 109
Arbor Company, 75
Atlantic Monthly, 47
attention to details,
 47–48
 admitting office, 51
 dealing with details,
  51–52
 inbound call center,
  52
 objects, forms,
  websites,
  systems,
  procedures, 52
 parking lot, 51
 service patrols, 52–53
 service walk and,
  48–50
Aurora St. Luke's, 75

Bacon, Francis, 83
Bain and Company, 13
Banco Popular, 80–82

Barksdale, Jim, 163
Berra, Yogi, 59
Berry, Leonard, 134, 185
Blanchard, Ken, 159
Brethower, Karen, 194
Bridges, Madeline, 201
Bringing Out the Best in
 Others!
 (Connellan), 191
Build-a-Bear Workshop,
 31
Business Week, 16, 17

Cabela's, 147–148
Campbell, David, 69
Carlzon, Jan, 53
celebrations
 contributor
  prominence,
  207
 functions of, 204
 guidelines, 208
 Hartsfield–Jackson
  Atlanta
  International
  Airport, 209
 human element of,
  207
 LensCrafters, 209
 manager role, 207
 Netflix, 208
 noteworthy, 208–209
 participants role, 207
 reasons for, 206
 special guests
  appearance, 207
 timing of, 205–206
Chip Bell Group, 76
Cisco, 114–115
Clark, Maxine, 31
Coming of Age in
 Samoa (Mead), 92
comment, complaint
 analysis, 33

compensation, benefits,
 16
Connellan, Tom, 191
Convergys, 87, 113
Costco, 16
Covey, Stephen, 217
cross-training, 17–18
customer advisory
 panels, 34
Customer Care Alliance,
 130
customer complaints, 38
 customer feedback
  solicitation, 44
 customer follow-up,
  44–45
 customer silence,
  39–40
 face-to-face listening,
  43
 frontline employees
  and, 44
 making it easier,
  43–45
 neutrality and, 45
 as opportunity, 43–44
 performance
  improvement
  and, 44
 stimulating
  complaints,
  40–42
 wants and all, 42–43
Customer Experience
 Report North
 America 2010, 41
customer forensics, lost
 customers
 alibis, 55
 lost customers, 54–55
 motive assessment
  and, 56–57
 opportunity and,
  55–56

customer loyalty,
    108–109
customer relations, 5,
    19–20
  customer satisfaction,
    21–22
  emotional aspects of,
    22–23
  employees and, 12–14
  measuring via
    customer-
    derived
    language, 24–26
  romancing the
    customer,
    customer
    intimacy, 26–27
  service quality and,
    13–14
customer relations,
    passion, 177
  affirmation, 180
  animation, 178–179
  appreciation, 179–180
  validation, 180–181
customer-focused
    management, see
    also management
  customer quality,
    104–105
  purpose and, 103
  technical quality,
    104–105
  think, 104–105

deal breakers, 48
DePree, Max, 218
Disney, 139
Donahue, John, 27, 115
Dueck, Rodney, 53

e is for excellence, 166
eBay, 27, 115
employee feedback. See
    also interpersonal
    feedback

confirm, correct, 190
  customers and, 191
  displaying, 191–194
  feedback system
    troubleshoo-ting,
    194–195
  graphic display of,
    193
  management of, 192
  to organization levels,
    193
  to person, team,
    192–193
  reporting, 192–193
  service goals and,
    191–192
  systems, 191
employee retention,
    see also hiring,
    recruiting
  compensation,
    benefits and, 16
  cross-training and,
    17–18
  customers and, 12–14
  empowerment and, 18
  experience and,
    12–13
  lateral job movement
    and, 18
  management and, 15
  productivity and, 13
  reward, recognition
    and, 18
  special contracts,
    perks, 17
  special treatment,
    16–17
  training and, 17
  turnover and, 16
employee training, 17
  administrative tasks,
    140
  Adoption Metaphor
    (ADOPT),
    142–143

anxiety reduction,
    141
  caution, 147
  competitive
    advantage, 145
  customer knowledge,
    148–149
  human resources
    (HR), line
    managers, 141
  implication, 146
  interpersonal skills,
    146–148
  making orientation
    work, 140–142
  new employee
    expectations, 141
  online forms,
    paperwork, 146
  orientation process,
    138–139
  people skills,
    146–147
  product, service
    knowledge, 148
  required skills,
    145–149
  right start, 137–138
  self-assessments, 147
  self-directed learning,
    147
  service successful
    organizations,
    144–145
  teamwork, 147
  technical skills, 146
  traditions course,
    139–140
  training department,
    formal training,
    149–150
empowerment, 18,
    161–169
  barriers to, 170–176
  permission and,
    174–175

proficiency, learning,
175–176
purpose and,
172–173
resistance to change,
173
responsible freedom
and, 171
risk factors and,
173–174
experience, 12–13

face-to-face listening,
30–31, 43
FedEx, 16, 37, 47, 172
Ferguson, Marilyn, 109
First Bank and Trust, 17
formal research, data
collection, 34
benchmarking, 37
customer surveys, 35
employee visit teams,
36
focus groups, 35
mystery shopping
services, 36
toll-free hotlines, 36
voice of the customer
(VOC) websites,
36
Forrester Research, 118
Fortune, 80
Freeman, Don, 74–75,
223
Fuller, Ed, 219

Gallup Organization, 23
Gates, Bill, 45, 57
Guiliani, Rudy, 47
grunt eyes, 46–47

Haller, Greg, 222
Hardee's, 171
Harris Interactive, 41
Hartsfield–Jackson
Atlanta

International
Airport, 209
*Harvard Business
Review,* 23, 88, 215
Heider, John, 200
hiring, recruiting, 1–2
active recruiting, 10
balancing efficiency
and effective-
ness, 4–5
casting tips, 6–11
employee flexibility,
6
job fit, 10
job previewing, 9
job-validated testing,
9
multiple interviews,
8
multiple selection
methods, 7
nontraditional
sources, 9–10
open roles, 6
peer interviews, 9
required skills, 7
roles *vs.* job, 5–6
screen test, 7
selection questions, 8
service-focused
companies, 3–4
Holmes, Oliver
Wendell, 224

incentives
customer link, 202
individual, team
recognition, 202
responsible freedom
affirmation,
202–203
tone of service match,
201–202
values outcome *vs.*
experience,
202–203

inspiration, 162
internet, online services
Convergys research,
113
customer partnering,
116, 119
customer per-
sonalization,
113–115
customer segments,
113
eBay, 115
Generation X,
millennials, 113
growth, 118
honesty, fairness,
115–118
live Web chat, 113
service diversity,
flexibility, 112
social media,
118–119
wireless and, 111
interpersonal feedback
clear feedback,
six steps,
199–200
ensuring feedback
heard, 197–198
forms of, 196–197
performance
standards and,
198
personal experience
and, 198
specific *vs.* open-
ended, 198–199
standards of, 196–197
winners and, 199
involvement, 161
Iverson, Ken, 169

James, William, 189

Koch, Ed, 190
Kurzweil, Larry, 220

lateral job movement, 18
layered group listening,
    31–33
leadership, coaching,
    211–212,
    see also service
    leadership in action
    boss to leader,
    151–152
    clipboards, whistles,
    152–153
    e is for excellence, 166
    empowerment,
    161–169
    evaluate, adjust,
    152–153
    failure, 155–156
    fundamentals, 152
    honesty and, 215
    leader respect, trust,
    215–216
    optimistic, 214–215
    performance,
    154–155
    performance,
    coaching
    technique
    match, 154–159
    preparing for success,
    153–154
    reinforce, motivate,
    153
    reprimands, 158–159
    on the sidelines, 153
    slumps, 156
    teamwork, 152
    trust and, 214–217
Leadership Is an Art
    (DePree), 218
Leider, Richard, 18
LensCrafters, 209
Levitt, Ted, 215
listening
    challenge of, 28–29
    comment, complaint
    analysis, 33

customer advisory
    panels, 34
    face-to-face, 30–31
    layered group
    listening, 31–33
    listen, understand,
    respond, 29–30
    multichannel
    response
    systems, 33
    online buzz
    monitoring,
    33–34
    six ways, customer
    needs and
    expectations,
    30–34
Longstreet, John, 92
lost customers, *see*
    customer forensics,
    lost customers
*The Loyalty Effect: The
    Hidden Force
    Behind Growth,
    Profits and Lasting
    Value* (Reichheld),
    13

Malcolm Baldrige
    National Quality
    Award, 71
management
    aggrieved customer
    and, 130–131
    of employee
    feedback, 192
    employee retention
    and, 15
    recognize, reward,
    incent, celebrate,
    185
Manheim, 75
Marriott, J. W., 11
Marriott Corporation,
    11, 115–116, 219
Mead, Margaret, 92, 93

mediocrity, 177–178
Microsoft, 186
multichannel response
    systems, 33

National Car Rental
    research, 128
National Hispanic
    University, 75–76
Nelson, Bob, 203
Netflix, 208
nonverbal cues, 111

Oliver, Tom, 129
One Minute Manager
    (Blanchard), 159
online buzz monitoring,
    33–34
Oren, John, 176
Orr, Barry, 17
Owl, Howland, 110

Park Nicollet Medical
    Centers, 53
passion for the
    customer, 177
    affirmation, 180
    animation, 178–179
    appreciation,
    179–180
    validation, 180–181
Peters, Tom, 212
Peterson, Robert,
    22–23
Pisano, Vic, 48
The Power of Purpose
    (Leider), 18
pressure, 5–6
Pritchett, Price, 181
productivity, 13

Quaker Steak and Lube,
    75
Quicken, 16
QVC Inc., 128

Raines, Jean, 216
recognize, reward,
    incent, celebrate,
    18
  definitions, 186
  employee needs,
    183–184
  favoritism, 188
  high-profile formal,
    186
  informal, 187
  lack of immediacy,
    188
  lasting value,
    188–189
  low-profile formal,
    186–187
  management and,
    185
  pitfalls, 187–188
  practice to program,
    186
  research, 186
  same old, 188
  winner takes all
    plans, 187–188
Reichheld, Fred, 13
RightNow.com, 41
Riley, Pat, 159
Ritz-Carlton Hotels,
    71–73
Riverside Health Care,
    216
Rockefeller, John D., 195

Sam's Club, 16
Scandinavian Airline
    Systems (SAS), 53
Schulze, Horst, 72, 143
Sea of Cortez
    (Steinbeck),
    108–109
*Service America in the
    New Economy*
    (Albrecht, Karl),
    101

service delivery process,
    85–86
  customer
    anthropology,
    effort, 88
  customer cultures
    and, 89
  customer language
    and, 90–91
  customer symbols
    and, 92
  customer time and,
    89
  customer traditions
    and, 91
  customer values and,
    90
Service delivery
    process, happy
  customer perspective
    and, 96–97
  defined, 95–96
  economics, return on
    investment and,
    97–98
  employee friendly, 99
  internal, external
    service, 97
  organization service
    vision and, 97
  process elimination,
    98
  process updating,
    customer
    expectations
    and, 98
  ten steps to creating,
    100–101
service failure, recovery,
    127
  aggrieved customer,
    131–133
  apologize, 129–130
  atonement, 130–131
  eliminate barriers,
    133

"fair fix" the problem,
    130
  follow up, 131
  frontline people and,
    133
  listen, empathize,
    130
  praise *vs.* critique,
    134
  promises, 131
  recovery defined,
    128–129
  support, encourage,
    134
  trained response,
    133
service leadership in
    action, 218
  adding value, 222
  connecting presence,
    219
  effective, 220–221
  employee support
    and, 220–221
  inspiration, 223
  listening practices,
    221
  meetings and,
    219–220
  optimism, tenacity
    strategy, 223
service standards, 77
  accountability, 82
  accuracy, 82
  communications, 81
  consistency, trust
    and, 82–83
  loyalty factors and,
    78–79
  moving target of,
    79–80
  people, 81
  responsiveness, 82
  standards, norms
    in action,
    80–82

service vision, 59–60
  crafting, 66–68
  customer aware
    cultures and, 64
  customer-centric
    cultures, 65–66
  customer-focused
    cultures, 65
  customer friendly
    organizations
    and, 64–65
  customer indifference
    and, 64
  employee focus and,
    68–69
  five customer
    strategies, 63–66
  power of service
    strategy, 61
  reliability and, 66–67
  service strategy
    choice, 62–66
  vision statement,
    67–68
service vision statement
  core contribution to
    customers, 74
  famous for what?, 74
  key customers and, 73
  key resources, 70
  no put-on at the Ritz,
    71
  sampler, 74–76
  words to action,
    73–74
  words with meaning,
    71

Smith, Fred, 37, 47, 172
special contracts, perks,
  17
special treatment, 16–17
standards,
  measurement, 102
  caution metrics, 107
  context metrics, 108
  correction metrics,
    107
  course metrics, 107
  customer and,
    105–106
  customer service
    dashboard,
    106–108
Starbucks, 16
Steinbeck, John, 108
Stringer, Hal, 126

The Tao of Leadership
  (Heider), 200
TARP Worldwide, 38–39
traditions course, 139
trust, 213
  honest leaders and,
    215
  keeping promises
    and, 216–217
  leader respect and,
    215–216
  optimistic leaders
    and, 214–215
turnover, 16

Universal Studios
  Hollywood, 220

value-addeds
  customer networks,
    125
  customer through
    difficult time,
    124
  customer who has
    thanked, 124
  customer with favor
    of complaining,
    123–124
  eight times to include,
    123–125
  first impressions,
    relationships,
    123
  going out of the way,
    125
  good deeds, 125
  new customers,
    124
  preplanned, 122
  salt-of-the-earth
    customers,
    123
  service magic,
    120–122
Verizon Wireless, 222

Wal-Mart, 16
Wilber, Philip, 150
Winfrey, Oprah, 209
wireless, 111
www.1to1media
  .com, 114

Zemke, Ron, 127

About the Authors

Chip R. Bell is a senior partner with The Chip Bell Group (CBG), headquartered near Atlanta. Prior to starting CBG in 1980, he was Director of Management Development for NCNB (now Bank of America). Dr. Bell is the author or coauthor of several best-selling books, including *Wired and Dangerous*, *Take Their Breath Away*, *Magnetic Service*, *Service Magic*, and *Customers as Partners*. He has appeared on CNBC, CNN, ABC, and FOX Business, and his work has been featured in *The Wall Street Journal*, *Fortune*, *USA Today*, *Fast Company*, and *Business Week*. A renowned keynote speaker, Chip has served as consultant or trainer to such organizations as Microsoft, USAA, Verizon, Cadillac, Marriott, Universal Orlando, Ritz-Carlton, Harley-Davidson, Accenture, Duke Energy, and Allstate.

Ron Zemke was one of the primary leaders of the American customer service revolution. His writings and research on the organizational impact of customer service are considered landmark. He was the first researcher in North America to write about the discipline of service management. Prior to Ron's untimely death in 2004, he authored or coauthored more than thirty five books including the best-selling *Service America in the New Economy*, the entire *Knock Your Socks Off Service* series, *E-Service, Generations at Work*, and *Service Magic: The Art of Amazing Your Customers*. He was Senior Editor of *Training* magazine, a syndicated columnist for the *American City Business Journals*, and the host of five films about the service management process.